"OUR COT WAS IN A FOREST GLADE."

Page 111

POEMS

BY

"HAPPY AT HOME."

Page 108

NEW-YORK

CLARK & AUSTIN.

1846.

POEMS,

BY

FRANCES S. OSGOOD.

A careless carol—idly, lightly sung,
  Perhaps not worth the singing or repeating;—
But would you check a woman's pen or tongue?—
  Ah! teach her first—to keep her heart from beating!

NEW YORK:
PUBLISHED BY CLARK & AUSTIN.

M DCCC XLVI.

Stereotyped by
RICHARD C. VALENTINE,
45 Gold-street, New York.

PECK & STAFFORD, Printers,
New Haven, Conn.

TO HER BEST FRIEND,

The following Pages

ARE AFFECTIONATELY AND GRATEFULLY INSCRIBED

BY

THE AUTHOR.

PREFACE.

The Author's chief fear, in collecting and publishing the following Poems, is that they may not be thought worthy the notice of that just and true criticism, whose praise and blame are alike valuable, and would by her be equally welcomed and appreciated.

CONTENTS.

POEMS.

TO THE SPIRIT OF POETRY.

Leave me not yet! Leave me not cold and lonely,
Thou dear Ideal of my pining heart!
Thou art the friend—the beautiful—the only,
Whom I would keep, tho' all the world depart!
Thou, that dost veil the frailest flower with glory,
Spirit of light and loveliness and truth!
Thou that didst tell me a sweet, fairy story,
Of the dim future, in my wistful youth!
Thou, who canst weave a halo round the spirit,
Thro' which naught mean or evil dare intrude,
Resume not yet the gift, which I inherit
From Heaven and thee, that dearest, holiest good!
Leave me not now! Leave me not cold and lonely,
Thou starry prophet of my pining heart!
Thou art the friend—the tenderest—the only,
With whom, of all, 'twould be despair to part.

Thou that cam'st to me in my dreaming childhood,
  Shaping the changeful clouds to pageants rare,
Peopling the smiling vale, and shaded wildwood,
  With airy beings, faint yet strangely fair ;
Telling me all the sea-born breeze was saying,
  While it went whispering thro' the willing leaves,
Bidding me listen to the light rain playing
  Its pleasant tune, about the household eaves ;
Tuning the low, sweet ripple of the river,
  Till its melodious murmur seem'd a song,
A tender and sad chant, repeated ever,
  A sweet, impassion'd plaint of love and wrong !
Leave me not yet ! Leave me not cold and lonely,
  Thou star of promise o'er my clouded path !
Leave not the life, that borrows from thee only
  All of delight and beauty that it hath !

Thou, that when others knew not how to love me,
  Nor cared to fathom half my yearning soul,
Didst wreathe thy flowers of light, around, above me,
  To woo and win me from my grief's control.
By all my dreams, the passionate, and holy,
  When thou hast sung love's lullaby to me,
By all the childlike worship, fond and lowly,
  Which I have lavish'd upon thine and thee.

By all the lays my simple lute was learning,
  To echo from thy voice, stay with me still!
Once flown—alas! for thee there's no returning!
  The charm will die o'er valley, wood, and hill.
Tell me not Time, whose wing my brow has shaded,
  Has wither'd spring's sweet bloom within my heart,
Ah, no! the rose of love is yet unfaded,
  Tho' hope and joy, its sister flowers, depart.

Well do I know that I have wrong'd thine altar,
  With the light offerings of an idler's mind,
And thus, with shame, my pleading prayer I falter,
  Leave me not, spirit! deaf, and dumb, and blind!
Deaf to the mystic harmony of nature,
  Blind to the beauty of her stars and flowers
Leave me not, heavenly yet human teacher,
  Lonely and lost in this cold world of ours!
Heaven knows I need thy music and thy beauty
  Still to beguile me on my weary way,
To lighten to my soul the cares of duty,
  And bless with radiant dreams the darken'd day:
To charm my wild heart in the worldly revel,
  Lest I, too, join the aimless, false, and vain;

Let me not lower to the soulless level
  Of those whom now I pity and disdain!
Leave me not yet!—leave me not cold and pining,
  Thou bird of paradise, whose plumes of light,
Where'er they rested, left a glory shining;
  Fly not to heaven, or let me share thy flight!

THE LUTIN-STEED.

A FAIRY LEGEND.

Old Margaret's wither'd features
  Gleam in the red firelight—
"Now stay with me, my grandsons three!
  Why wend ye forth to-night?

"The Mistral's mighty wing—
  Hark! how it shakes the roof!
This eve the fairy Sabbath is,
  And *souls* should keep aloof.

"The Lutins are abroad,
In thousand forms of might,
To mock the feeble faith of man;—
Ye shall not forth to-night!"

Out spake the eldest proudly,
And toss'd his cluster'd curls,—
"I go to meet my Jacqueline,
My blue-eyed girl of girls!"

Out spake the second loudly,
"Nor Lutin, elf, or fay,
Shall keep me from the beach to-night,
Where foams the flashing spray!"

"And thou, my fair-hair'd darling!
My beautiful and bright!
Of stories fine, great store have I,
Thou wilt not forth to-night?"

"Nay, grandam!" lisp'd the loved one,
With playful, pleading look,
"Thy legends keep, till I come back,
With blossoms from the brook!"

* * * * * * * *
* * * * * * * *

"They're gone!" old Margaret murmur'd,
And fierce the Mistral blew,
And spirit voices echo'd round,
"Gone! gone!" the long night through!—

* * * * * * * *
* * * * * * * *

"She talk'd of wind and tempest,"
The careless wanderers cried,—
"Now never walk'd the moon in heaven,
With more resplendent pride!

"Ha! there's old Caspar's horse,
His mane like midnight flows,
Mount! mount! away, my little steed!
How gallantly he goes!

"He'll bear us to the fountain;
We'll have a glorious ride!"
"Oh! brothers dear—I fear—I fear!"
The youthful Adolphe cried,—

"He goes not to the fountain—
I hear the sea-waves roar—
And hark! the tempest raves above—
And see—the rain doth pour!

"Oh! turn him!—turn him homeward!
How wild—how fast he flies!
It is—it is—a Lutin-steed!
And he who rides him—dies!"

They strove in vain to turn him,
They strove to check his speed;—
The lightning glares!—the thunder howls
Around the demon-steed!—

The ocean heaves before him—
He neighs with fiendish joy—
His flaming hoofs have touch'd the beach—
Heaven save that hapless boy!

The cold waves kiss their white lips,
And deeper yet they go;
The cold waves close above their heads,—
And drown that shriek of wo!—

* * * * * * * *
* * * * * * * *
* * * * * * * *

The maiden at her lattice,—
The grandam at her door,—
And morning on the misty hills!—
But they come never more!

LOVE'S REPLY.

I'll tell you something chanced to me,
(A quaint and simple story,)
Before I cross'd, with dreaming heart
Old ocean's gloom and glory.

Around me came three graceful girls,
Their farewell whisper breathing,—
Julie,—with light and lovely curls,
Her snowy shoulders wreathing;

And proud Georgine,—with stately mien,
  And glance of calm hauteur,
Who moves—a Grace,—and looks—a queen,
  All passionless and pure ;

And Kate, whose low, melodious tone
  Is tuned by Truth and Feeling,
Whose shy yet wistful *eyes* talk on,
  When fear her *lips* is sealing.

" From what far country shall I write ?"
  I ask'd, with pride elated,
" From what rare monument of art
  Shall be my letters dated ?"

Julie toss'd back her locks of light,
  With girlish grace and glee,—
" To me from glorious Venice write,
  Queen-city of the Sea !"

" And thou, Georgine ?" Her dark eyes flash'd,—
  " Ah ! date to me your lines
From some proud palace, where the pomp
  Of olden Honor shines !"

But Kate,—the darling of my soul,
  My bright, yet bashful flower,
In whose dear heart some new, pure leaf,
  Seems to unfold each hour,—

Kate turn'd her shy, sweet looks from mine,
  Lest I her blush should see,
And said—so only Love could hear—
  "Write from your *heart* to *me!*"

THE FAN.

A LOVER'S FANTASY.

Dainty spirit, that dost lie
Couch'd within the zephyr's sigh,
Murmur in mine earnest ear
Music of the starry sphere!
Softest melody divine
Lend unto each lyric line,

Till the lay of love shall seem
Light and airy as its theme.

Ah! not unto mortal wight
Wilt thou whisper, frolic sprite!
Fancy! wave *thy* fairy wing,
While the magic Fan I sing!

Airy minister of Fate,
On whose meaning motions wait
Half an hundred butterflies,
Idle beaux—more fond than wise—
Basking in the fatal smile
That but wins them to beguile!
Blest be they who fashion'd thee,
Beauty's graceful toy to be!
Virgin gold from Orient cave—
Veinėd pearl from ocean's wave—
Showing like her temples fair
Through her curls of lustrous hair—
Tints of richest glow and light
From a master's palette bright,
On the parchment rarely wrought,
Till the painting *life* has caught,—

All have made thee plaything fit,
For a maiden's grace and wit.
She can teach thee witchery's spell,
Make thy lightest motion *tell*,
Bid thee speak, though mute thou art,
All the language of the heart.

When her eyes say softly "yes,"
Thou canst hide and yet express
All the enchanting blush would speak
While it warms her modest cheek,
And thy motion well can show,
With one flutter to or fro,
Her disdain's indignant "no."

Queen of fans! the downy pressure
Of her snow-white, dimpled hand,
As it clasps the costly treasure,
Wrought in India's glowing land,
Has it not a *soul* impress'd
On the toy by her caress'd?

Ah! what ministry divine,
Frail, yet love-taught fan, is thine!

Thou shouldst be a beauteous bird,
Flying at her lightest word,
Nestling near her silken zone,
Like a gem on Beauty's throne,
Or a young aerial sprite
Watching every smile of light:
Art thou not? Methinks I trace,
Now and then, an angel face
Gleaming, as thy painted wing
Flies before her—happy thing!
Sometimes I could almost swear
Love himself had hidden there,
Aiming thence his shafts of fire,
Now in sport and now in ire.
Hearts obey each proud behest
By thy lightest touch express'd,
As thou glancest to and fro,
Fluttering in her hand of snow.
So, fair spirit, fold thy wing
While thy ministry I sing!
Softly wave each careless curl
O'er her brow—the radiant girl;
Fan each pure and precious tint
Feeling on her cheek doth print;

Wake it from its pure repose,
Till the dear blush comes and goes;
Shade the dimple's frolic grace
Sporting o'er her sunny face;
Hide the smile of playful scorn
From her spirit's buoyance born;
Veil the timid sigh that parts,
Trembling, from her "heart of hearts;"
Aid the glances—words of light—
Flashing from her eye's blue night,
And her dearest bidding do,
Like an Ariel fond and true!

All sweet airs and incense wait
On thy wave, fair wand of Fate!
Soft and balmy, as her sigh,
  Be each zephyr thou dost wake,
Round her graceful head to fly,
  Blest be thou for Beauty's sake!

Yet, oh spirit! fold thy wing,
While thy ministry I sing!
Show her how some touch, too bold,
Marr'd thy robe of pearl and gold;

Whisper as thou wavest by,
Beauty's light like thine will die
If she waste its bloom divine
On the idlers round her shrine;
Warn her that *her* spirit's wing
Be not ever fluttering;
For if *that* should break, or show
Lightest shade upon its snow,
Lives no mortal artisan
That can make it bright again!
Tears may bathe the broken plume,
Sighs may mourn its early doom—
Only may it hope for *rest*
Folded on the Father's breast.

So, fair spirit, wave thy wing,
And my message softly sing!
"Do thy spiriting gently" there,
Lest thou wound a soul so rare,
And be this the warning dear
Murmur'd in her ivory ear—

"Lovely lady, have a care!
Words are more than idle air,

Smiles can surer wound or heal
Than the stars, whose light they steal.
She whose power is undenied
Should have pity with her pride,
Should remember, while her frown
Clouds the hope she may not crown,
Rarest skill and subtlest art
Cannot mend the *broken heart!*"
So, fair spirit, wave thy wing,
And thy warning softly sing!

TO SYBIL.

"Sooth her in sorrow and brighten her smile;
Chide her most gently if folly beguile;
One so unsullied and trustful of heart,
From the good shepherd will never depart.

"Now she adores thee as one without spot,
Dreams not of sorrow to darken her lot.
Joyful, yet tearful, I yield her to thee;
Take her, the light of thy dwelling to be."

Yes! go to him—thy young heart full
Of passionate romance,
And be the fiat of thy fate
His lordly word and glance!

Be thy soul's day, his careless smile;
His frown, its clouded night;
His voice, the music of thy life;
His love, thy one delight!

Sit at his feet, and raise to his
  Those large, pure, dreaming eyes,
And tell him all thy lovely thoughts
  As radiantly they rise.

Press to his hand that childish cheek,
  And stroke his stern dark face,
And charm him with thy ways so meek,
  Thy glad, aerial grace!

Look for his coming with clasp'd hands
  And hush'd and listening heart,
And strive to hide thy joyous tears
  With woman's bashful art.

And in thy low Eolian tones,
  Melodiously wild,
Falter thy fond, sweet welcome out,
  Oh, rare, enchanting child!

Then if he coldly turn away,
  In silence to him steal,
And touch his soul with one long gaze
  Of passionate appeal.

I know them all—th' endearing wiles—
  The sweet, unconscious art—
The graceful spells that nature taught
  Her darling's docile heart.

I know them all—I've seen thee lift,
  At some unkindly tone,
Those dark, upbraiding eyes of thine,
  Where sorrowing wonder shone,

And sudden tears would dim the glance,
  And then—the wrong forgiven—
A smile would steal up in the cloud,
  Like starlight into heaven.

Go—try them all—those girlish wiles!
  He cannot choose but love,
He cannot choose but guard from ill
  His little, nestling dove!

For rare, my Sybil, 'tis to see
  Thy iris-mind unfold;
The magic of thy maiden glee,
  That turns all gloom to gold;—

Th' aurora blush that on thy cheek
  Thy heart's love-story tells ;
The wondrous world within thine eyes
  Lit up like the gazelle's.

But if thou think'st, dear dreaming child !
  That he will watch as now,
In after years, each smile and shade
  That cross thy changing brow ;

And modulate his tone to meet
  The pleading of thy soul,
And feel in all his wanderings,
  Thy gentle breast his goal ;

And daily feed thy mind and heart
  With hallow'd love and lore,
Nor turn from those imploring eyes,
  That wistful look for more ;

And watch thee where—as borne in air—
  Thou float'st the dance along,
And deem thy form alone is fair,
  Of all the fairy throng ;

In transport look and listen when
  Thy light caressing hands
Lure forth the harp's harmonious soul,
  From all its silver bands ;

Indulgent stoop his falcon-will
  To let it fly with thine,
And smile in manly pride to see
  His pet's soft plumage shine ;

And yield to every gay caprice,
  And grieve for every sigh,
And grant all airy hopes that play
  On pleading lip or eye ;

If *this* thy dream, enthusiast, be,
  I can but idly pray,
Heaven shield thee in thy *waking* hour,
  And keep it long away !

A FLIGHT OF FANCY.

At the bar of Judge Conscience, stood Reason ar-
raign'd,
The Jury impannell'd—the prisoner chain'd.
The Judge was facetious, at times, though severe,
Now waking a smile, and now drawing a tear;
An old-fashion'd, fidgety, queer-looking wight,
With a clerical air, and an eye quick as light.

"Here, Reason, you vagabond! look in my face;
I'm told you're becoming an idle scapegrace.
They say that young Fancy, that airy coquette,
Has dared to fling round you her luminous net;
That she ran away with you, in spite of yourself,
For pure love of frolic—the mischievous elf.

"The scandal is whisper'd by friends and by foes,
And darkly they hint too, that when they propose

Any question to *your* ear, so lightly you're led,
At once to gay Fancy, you turn your wild head;
And *she* leads you off in some dangerous dance,
As wild as the Polka that gallop'd from France.

"Now up to the stars with you, laughing, she springs,
With a whirl and a whisk of her changeable wings;
Now dips in some fountain her sun-painted plume,
That gleams thro' the spray, like a rainbow in bloom;
Now floats in a cloud, while her tresses of light
Shine through the frail boat and illumine its flight;
Now glides through the woodland to gather its flowers;
Now darts like a flash to the sea's coral bowers;
In short—cuts such capers, that with her I ween
It's a wonder you are not ashamed to be seen!

"Then she talks such a language!—melodious enough,
To be sure—but a strange sort of outlandish stuff!
I'm told that it licenses many a whapper,
And when once she commences no frowning can stop her;

Since it's new—I've no doubt it is very improper!
They say that she cares not for order or law;
That of you—you great dunce!—she but makes a cat's paw.
I've no sort of objection to fun in it's season,
But it's plain that this Fancy is *fooling* you, Reason!"

Just then into court flew a strange little sprite,
With wings of all colors and ringlets of light!
She frolick'd round Reason—till Reason grew wild,
Defying the court and caressing the child.
The judge and the jury, the clerk and recorder,
In vain call'd this exquisite creature to order:—
"Unheard of intrusion!"—They bustled about,
To seize her, but, wild with delight, at the rout,
She flew from their touch like a bird from a spray,
And went waltzing and whirling and singing away!

Now up to the ceiling, now down to the floor!
Were never such antics in courthouse before!
But a lawyer, well versed in the tricks of his trade,
A trap for the gay little innocent laid:
He held up a *mirror*, and Fancy was caught

By her image within it, so lovely, she thought.
What could the fair creature be!—bending its eyes
On her own with so wistful a look of surprise!
She flew to embrace it. The lawyer was ready:
He closed round the spirit a grasp cool and steady,
And she sigh'd, while he tied her two luminous wings,
"Ah! Fancy and Falsehood are different things!"

The witnesses—maidens of uncertain age,
With a critic, a publisher, lawyer and sage—
All scandalized greatly at what they had heard,
Of this poor little Fancy, (who flew like a bird!)
Were call'd to the stand and their evidence gave:
The judge charged the jury, with countenance grave.
Their verdict was "guilty," and Reason look'd down,
As his honor exhorted her thus, with a frown:—

"This Fancy, this vagrant, for life shall be chain'd,
In your own little cell, where *you* should have remain'd;
And you—for *your* punishment—jailer shall be:
Don't let your accomplice come coaxing to me!
I'll none of her nonsense—the little wild witch!
Nor her bribes—although rumor does say she is rich.

"I've heard that all treasures and luxuries rare,
Gather round at her bidding, from earth, sea, and
air;
And some go so far as to hint, that the powers
Of darkness attend her more sorrowful hours.
But go!" and Judge Conscience, who never was
bought,
Just bow'd the pale prisoner out of the court.

'Tis said,—that poor Reason next morning was
found,
At the door of her cell, fast asleep on the ground,
And nothing within, but one plume rich and rare,
Just to show that young Fancy's wing once had been
there.
She had dropp'd it, no doubt, while she strove to get
through
The hole in the lock, which she could not undo.

THE HEART'S ANSWER.

A SONG.

"Speak—speak to me, darling!
  Hide thy sweet blush in my breast;
Breathe but one dear little murmur;
  Thine eyes shall tell me the rest.

"Say only thou wilt be mine, love;
  Whisper me one little—'Yes!'
Ah! thou art silent,—thy soul, love,
  Feels not my pleading caress!"

Low as the sigh of a flower,
  Heard in the stillness of night,
Came the fond tones of the maiden,
  Trembling with fear and delight,—

" Ask not the word from my lips, love ;
  Need'st thou so idle a sign !
Dost thou not hear my *heart* answer,
  Thus beating softly on thine ?"

LOVE'S MISTAKE

On mission pure, from realms divine,
Young Love was sent to Virtue's shrine,
But, wild and gay, he " stopp'd to play"
With sportive Beauty by the way.

She led him thro' her balmy bowers,
She chain'd him with a wreath of flowers,
She charm'd him with her magic smile,
And softly murmur'd—" Rest awhile !"

Alas ! his sight is blinded quite,
By Beauty's dazzling glance of light ;

And while the wily siren sings,
The boy forgets his angel-wings!

Yet still he sometimes leaves his play,
And asks to Virtue's shrine the way;
But Beauty weaves anew her chain,
And Virtue looks for Love in vain.

TO A DEAR LITTLE TRUANT,

Who wouldn't come home.

When are you coming? the flowers have come!
Bees in the balmy air happily hum;
In the dim woods where the cool mosses are,
Gleams the Anemone's little, light star;
Tenderly, timidly down in the dell,
Sighs the sweet violet, droops the harebell;—
Soft in the wavy grass lightens the dew;
Spring keeps her promises,—why do not *you?*

Up in the blue air, the clouds are at play,—
You are more graceful and lovely than they;
Birds in the branches sing all the day long,
When are you coming to join in their song?
Fairer than flowers, and fresher than dew!
Other sweet things are here,—why are not *you?*

Why don't you come? we have welcomed the Rose!
Every light zephyr, as gayly it goes,
Whispers of *other* flowers, met on its way,
Why has it nothing of *you*, love, to say?
Why does it tell us of music and dew?
Rose of the South! we are waiting for *you!*

Do not delay, darling, 'mid the dark trees,
"Like a lute" murmurs the musical breeze;
Sometimes the brook, as it trips by the flowers,
Hushes its warble to listen for yours.
Pure as the rivulet,—lovely and true!
Spring should have waited till she could bring *you!*

LULU.

There's many a maiden
  More brilliant, by far,
With the step of a fawn,
  And the glance of a star;
But heart there was never
  More tender and true,
Than beats in the bosom
  Of darling Lulu!

Her eyes are too modest
  To dazzle; but oh!
They win you to love her,
  If *you* will or no!
And when they glance up,
  With their shy, startled look,
Her soul trembles in them,
  Like light in a brook.

There are bright eyes by thousands,
  Black, hazel, and blue ;
But whose are so loving
  As those of Lulu !

And waves of soft hair,
  That a poet would vow
Was moonlight on marble,
  Droop over her brow.
The rose rarely blooms
  Thro' that light, silken maze,
But when it does play there,
  How softly it plays !
Oh ! there's many a maiden
  More brilliant, 'tis true,
But none so enchanting
  As little Lulu !

She flits, like a fairy,
  About me all day,
Now nestling beside me,
  Now up and away !
She singeth unbidden,
  With warble as wild

As the lay of the meadow-lark,
  Innocent child!
She's playful, and tender,
  And trusting, and true,
She's sweet as a lily,
  My dainty Lulu!

She whispers sweet fancies,
  Now mournful, now bright,
Then deepen her glances,
  With love and delight;
And the slow, timid smile,
  That dawns in her face,
Seems fill'd with her spirit's
  Ineffable grace.
Oh! the world cannot offer
  A treasure so true,
As the childlike devotion
  Of happy Lulu!

A REPLY

TO ONE WHO SAID, "WRITE FROM YOUR HEART.

Ah! woman still
Must veil the shrine,
Where feeling feeds the fire divine,
Nor sing at will,
Untaught by art,
The music prison'd in her heart!

Still gay the note,
And light the lay,
The woodbird warbles on the spray,
Afar to float;
But homeward flown,
Within his nest, how changed the tone!

Oh! none can know,
Who have not heard
The music-soul that thrills the bird,

The carol low,
As coo of dove
He warbles to his woodland-love!

The world would say
'Twas vain and wild,
Th' impassion'd lay of Nature's child;
And Feeling, so
Should veil the shrine,
Where softly glow her fires divine!

TO MY MOTHER.

SWEET mother! you fear while no longer you guide
me,
The Past will be lost in the Present's gay show;
But ah! whether joy or misfortune betide me,
I love you too dearly, *your* love to forego!

I would not, for all that the Future can bring me,
  Forget the dear hours when I sat at your feet,
The song, that was sure of approval to sing thee,
  The look, that was always so loving to meet.

When I flew to your smile with each joyous emotion,
  But hid from your heart every sorrow I knew ;—
Oh ! wayward perhaps was my childish devotion ;
  But it ne'er for a moment was cold or untrue.

And still, when the chill wing of wo darkens o'er me,
  I am grateful its shadow extends not to thee ;
While if Praise thrill my heart or if joy smile before me,
  I sigh—" Could *she* know it, how glad she would be !"

Sweet mother ! too fondly your darling you cherish'd,
  For me to forget you, wherever I go,—
Ah no ! not till memory's power has perish'd ;
  I love you too dearly to turn from you so !

THE BROKEN LYRE.

A DAINTY lyre was lent to Joy,
A simple, frail, but treasured toy ;—
And gaily sweet its tones were heard,
As warble of a wandering bird.

A blooming boy from distant clime
Came by and caught its silvery chime,
He coax'd from Joy his fragile lyre,
And swept the strings with hand of fire.

Ah ! wo the day—that reckless child
Awoke the chords with will so wild !
One pleading, passionate strain he play'd,
And broke the lyre, that Heaven had made !

Ah ! wo the day—that stranger sprite
Attuned to grief the plaything light,
And strain'd its chords with childish art !—
The boy was Love—the lyre a heart !

GOLDEN RULES IN RHYME.

FROM A MATRON TO A MAIDEN.

"While I touch the string,
  Wreathe my brows with laurel;
For the song I sing
  Has for once a moral!"—Moore.

Come listen, while in careless rhyme,
  Some golden rules I give you
That you may hoard the wealth of Time,
  And life may not deceive you.

In childhood's hours, when in the sun
  Our sportive group assembled,
And off our frail pipes, one by one,
  The glittering bubbles trembled;

If mine with lovelier lustre shone,
  Or higher soar'd,—what trouble!
My brother, leaving all *his own*,
  Blew out my beaming bubble!

And thus the world—when young Romance
  Her airy dreams is weaving,
And Hope's soft rainbows round them dance,
  As radiant, as deceiving,

Thus will the world, my child, destroy,
  With treachery more refined,
The soaring dreams of love and joy,
  The bubbles of the mind!

Then yet in time a lesson learn,
  From one who learn'd too late,
That world, whose laugh *we* laugh to scorn,
  Her fiat *here* is fate!

When honor, placed in reason's scales,
  Outweighs THE OWL'S opinion,
All free and fearless, trim your sails,
  And steer for Heaven's dominion!

But still in trifles, where no wrong
  Can come of yielding to her,
Oh! chord with hers your careless song,
  And of her smiles be sure!

When Love would fling his flowery net
  Around your joyous spirit,
Ask not for rank, or wealth, or wit,
  But yield to manly merit.

Remember—Love but seldom strings
  His flowers on *golden* wire,
Remember—Wit has wanton wings,
  That *might* put out his fire.

Your heart be like a stainless glass,
  Where fleeting, outward graces
But lend their beauty as they pass,
  And leave behind no traces;

On which—its subtle nature's such,
  The gem of gems—in glory—
The diamond, with its lightning touch.
  Alone can write love's story.

As to the moon, the ocean's tide
  Subjects its strength unruly,
So let a light from Heaven, love, guide
  The tide of passion truly.

If sorrow come—resist it not,
  Nor yet bow weakly to it;
Look up to meet the Heaven-sent storm;
  But see the rainbow thro' it!

And let not pleasure's reckless hands
  Too often shake time's glass, love:
At best, the few and priceless sands
  Too surely, swiftly pass, love!

And seek not bliss on airy heights,
  Where dizzy power doth rally!
The "fragrant little heart's-ease" lights
  The lowliest, humblest valley.

The gem that clasps a royal robe
  The worldling's eye may dazzle,
But Love will light his glow-worm lamp
  In cot as well as castle.

The magic flower in Erin's Isle,
  That bears about a blessing,
Perchance is but good-humor's smile,
  A kindly heart's caressing.

If comes a blow, from friend or foe,
  With earnest good avenge it,
" The sandal-tree, with fragrant sigh,
  Perfumes the axe that rends it."

Be like the sun, whose eye of joy
  Ne'er on a shadow lay, love !
Be like the rill that singeth still,
  Whate'er be in its way, love !

Ne'er waste your heart in vain regret,
  Tho' youth be dimm'd by care ;
" For lovelier flowers than summer wreathes
  May twine in winter's hair."

With childlike trust look forward still,
  For Heaven is always near ;
" Full oft our very fear of ill
  Exceeds the ill we fear."

Nor question Fate ! the world-ship still
  Under seal'd orders sailing ;
'Twere best the great Commander's skill
  To trust with faith unfailing.

Nor idly waste the golden hours,
  The plumes of Time's swift wings:
The watch must still be wound to work,
  Or rust corrodes its springs.

If once a purpose pure and high
  You form, for naught forego it!
"The mulberry leaf to silk is changed
  By Patience," says the poet.

Let Fancy fly her fairy kite,
  And light with wit its wing, dear;
But oh, lest it go out of sight,
  Bid Reason hold the string, dear.

For, soaring where the poet's heaven
  With starry gems is spangled,
It might, by Folly's zephyr driven,
  In *moonshine* get entangled.

Yet sneer not thou at those who rise
  To loftier delusions;
"Great truths are oft," the sage replies,
  "Foreshadow'd by illusions."

Confide in Friendship's right good-will,
But not too often task it;
"It is the highest price we pay
For any thing, to *ask* it."

If Nature's glorious overture
Discordant seem to be, love,
Be sure your *heart* is out of tune,
And try the sounding key, love!

Let more than the domestic mill
Be turned by Feeling's river;
Let Charity "*begin* at home,"
But not *stay* there forever.

Look on the poor with pitying eyes,
And "reason not the *need*;"
For angels in that mean disguise
May often ask their meed.

But if a debt by honor seal'd
Uncancell'd yet remain,
Oh, ne'er to generous impulse yield
What Justice asks in vain!

Be frank and pure, and brave and true,—
  True to thyself and Heaven ;
And be thy friends, the gifted few ;
  And be thy foes forgiven.

And hold thyself so dear, so high,
  That evil come not near thee,
That meanness dare not meet thine eye,
  And Falsehood fly and fear thee !

Shrink not to aim the shafts of wit,
  At all that's mean or narrow ;
But oh, before you bend the bow,
  Be sure it holds the arrow !

Command your temper, guard your tongue,
  Lest they have sway undue ;
For deeds, not words, the bell be rung,
  Which fame may ring for you !

And so, if from my careless rhyme,
  You cull the rose of Reason,
I have not wasted all my time,
  But said " a word in season."

A SONG.

Call me pet names, dearest! Call me a bird,
That flies to thy breast at one cherishing word,
That folds its wild wings there, ne'er dreaming of
flight,
That tenderly sings there in loving delight!
Oh! my sad heart keeps pining for one fond
word,—
Call me pet names, dearest! Call me thy bird!

Call me sweet names, darling! Call me a flower,
That lives in the light of thy smile each hour,
That droops when its heaven—thy heart—grows
cold,
That shrinks from the wicked, the false and bold,
That blooms for thee only, through sunlight and
shower;
Call me pet names, darling! Call me thy flower!

Call me fond names, dearest! Call me a star,
Whose smile's beaming welcome thou feel'st from afar,
Whose light is the clearest, the truest to thee,
When the "night-time of sorrow" steals over life's sea:
Oh! trust thy rich bark, where its warm rays are,
Call me pet names, darling! Call me thy star!

Call me dear names, darling! Call me thine own!
Speak to me always in Love's low tone!
Let not thy look nor thy voice grow cold:
Let my fond worship thy being enfold;
Love me forever, and love me alone!
Call me pet names, darling! Call me thine own!

THE SPIRIT'S VOYAGE.

"When the child was buried, a little canoe with a sail to it, laden with bread-fruit and cocoas, was sent off from the shore with a fair wind, in order, as they said, to bear the spirit of the dead away from the land of the living."

"THEY'VE fill'd with fruit their frail canoe,
With fruit and flowers of brilliant hue,
A blooming freight—but whose the hand
To guide the light thing from the land?
So feathery light,—'twould seem a sin
To trust a fairy's weight within.
The waves are bright,—the skies are fair,—
A balmy blessing is the air,—
Her sail is set,—she glides away!
Where goes the graceful boat to-day?
I hear no voice come o'er the tide;
I see no form the helm beside;
And it might seem a moment's toy,

But that they wear no smile of joy,
And fondly watch its snowy wing,
As if it were a holy thing :—
Why send they forth their boat to be
A plaything for the reckless sea?"
"Oh, stranger! calm or wild the tide,
Their light canoe will safely glide,
And all unscathed by tempest-shock,
By coral-reef or roughest rock,
Ere morn, its white sail will be furl'd
Forever in the spirit-world.
A viewless hand that bark obeys,
A voice unheard the sea-wave sways,
A thing so holy and so fair,
Serene and safe, is smiling there,
That fiercest winds before it falter,
And into harmless zephyrs alter.
Ah! well may they the wanderer mark;
For know,—within that blessed bark,
The spirit of a little child
Is playing on the waters wild!
Behold our chieftain's burial-ground!
We raised to-day another mound.
Behold its lone and hallow'd tree!
So graceful and so fair was she.

But look!—the boat is seen no more;
The mourning train have left the shore;
And, hark! those accents sad and wild!
Our island chief laments his child."

THE LAMENT.

No more!—ah! never, never more!
  Her precious feet will tread,
Like light, our dwelling's coral floor,*
  By young affection led;

Those little feet, whose graceful fall,
  So airy and so gay,
Broke not the frailest shell of all
  That glitter'd in her way.

No more! Ah! never, never more,
  Her glancing hands will braid
Our painted mats to shade the door,
  Where warm the noontide play'd!

* The floor of the hut is strewed with fragments of coral and shell.

No more with lightest limbs she'll spring
  Far up the cocoa-tree,
No more the cocoa-cup she'll bring,
  With sunny smile to me!

But safer, through the land of souls,
  Those tender feet shall go,
And where the endless river rolls,
  More rich the cocoas grow;

And still beneath her joyous hand
  The spirit-fruit shall rise,
Forever blooming through the land,
  Where *nothing* droops and dies!

Her dark hair's long and glossy stream,
  Shall bright kahullahs deck;
And wreaths of rainbow shells shall gleam
  Around her arms and neck.

Play on amid those fragrant bowers,
  My fair and happy child!
Ere long another bark of ours
  Shall brave the waters wild;

And though 'twould scarce—a boat so weak,
The *sin-weigh'd* soul, sustain,
A father's spirit cannot seek
His only child *in vain!*

A REMONSTRANCE.

WRITTEN AT THE CATSKILL MOUNTAIN HOUSE.

WHAT, here! where the soul feels an angel's elation,
Where the balm of the breeze is worth all the world's wealth!
Oh! profane not the place by so low a libation,
While pure from the rock springs the fountain of health!

What, here! where the wood-bird its warble subduing,
Keeps holy our Sabbath with music and love,
And Earth, her wild blossoms forever renewing,
Sends up, in their perfume, her praises above!

Where the skies seem to bend, in their luminous beauty,
So loving and low o'er the green mountain-sod,
That the spirit, attuned to devotion and duty,
Sees Nature embracing her Father and God!

No temple can match, with a glory so solemn,
The forest-cathedral that rises around;
The pine's stately shaft, for the fair marble column,
All vein'd with the sunlight, and gracefully crown'd;

Its dome—the unlimited arch, glowing o'er us;
Its censer—yon budding spray, swung by the breeze;
Its music—the hymn of the fountain before us;
Its light—Heaven's smile—stealing soft through the trees:

And oh! the bright treasures around and below us,
The buds of the wild mountain-laurel, behold!
So perfect, so gem-like! where, where will you show us
A richer mosaic in temple of old?

Profane not the place by so base a libation!
Look around ye—look upward! and drink if ye dare!
Away with the wine-cup, the curse of creation!
Yon fount has enough for us all, and to spare.

"BOIS TON SANG, BEAUMANOIR!"*

FIERCE raged the combat—the foemen press'd nigh,
When from young Beaumanoir rose the wild cry,
Beaumanoir, 'mid them all, bravest and first,
"Give me to drink, for I perish of thirst!"
Hark! at his side, in the deep tones of ire,
"Bois ton SANG, Beaumanoir!" shouted his sire!

Deep had it pierced him—the foemen's swift sword—
Deeper his soul felt the wound of that word!

* The incident is related in Froissart's Chronicles.

Back to the battle, with forehead all flush'd,
Stung to wild fury, the noble youth rush'd!
Scorn in his dark eyes—his spirit on fire—
Deeds were his answer that day to his sire.
Still where triumphant the young hero came,
Glory's bright garland encircled his name;
But in her bower, to beauty a slave,
Dearer the guerdon his lady-love gave,
While on his shield that no shame had defaced,
"Bois ton sang, Beaumanoir!" proudly she traced!

THE LILY'S DELUSION.

A COLD, calm star look'd out of heaven,
And smiled upon a tranquil lake,
Where, pure as angel's dream at even,
A Lily lay but half awake.

The flower felt that fatal smile
And lowlier bow'd her conscious head;

"Why does he gaze on me the while?"
The light, deluded Lily said.

Poor dreaming flower!—too soon beguiled,
She cast nor thought nor look elsewhere,
Else she had known the star but smiled
To see himself reflected there.

THE FETTER 'NEATH THE FLOWERS.

Cupid flung his garland gaily
O'er a maid in seeming play;—
Sage Experience whisper'd daily,
"Break the chain, while yet you may!"

"Why?" she cried—"'tis but a toy,
Form'd of many a fragrant flower;
Let me still its bloom enjoy,—
I can break it any hour."

Long she sported freely, lightly,
  With her soft and glowing chain ;—
" Nay ! it clasps my heart so tightly,
  I must break the toy in twain."

Vain resolve !—the tie that bound her,
  Harden'd 'neath her struggling will ;
Fast its *blossoms* fell around her,
  But the fetter linger'd still.

TO ——

They tell me in Fashion's illumined saloon,
Where the dance lightly echoes the melody's tune,
Where Beauty and Grace weave the spell of delight,
And the waltz and mazourka mock Time in his flight,
Where they crown the gay hours with rarest of
    flowers,
No forms floating there are more lovely than yours ;
That the brightest of balls wants a charm and a grace,
If *your* eyes refuse their soft light to the place.

I seek not—I love not the balls of the gay,
Where my lone spirit pines for its dear ones away;
I see not your beauty when deck'd for the dance,
When blossom and gem mock the blush and the
glance;
You come not to me in the glow of your pride,
For you know I've a welcome, but nothing beside;
Yet you bring me a smile that is sweeter by far
Than the gay one whose light is the festival's star;
While with heart full of love, as your hands are of
toys,
You bless sunny childhood by sharing its joys.
Oh! dearer its innocent rapture than all
The praises that follow the belle of the ball;
And you seem at such moments more graceful to me,
Than you would when array'd for the festival's glee.

TO SARAH,

ARRANGING HER HAIR.

OH, rich in *heart!* what matter how
The silken tresses shade your brow?
What matter, whether gem or rose,
  Or simple riband wreathe your hair,
While that soft blush so purely glows,
  While those dark eyes such beauty wear?

No rich array could lend your form,
Thus airy-light, one added charm;
No jewel gift that girlish face
With lovelier glow or softer grace;
And he who looks on you with eyes,
Where all his soul to yours replies,
Is prouder of you simply so,
Than when adorn'd your graces glow;
And joys to know his fairy flower

Can gayly bloom in Home's sweet bower,
While some, less fair, the hot-house air
Of Flattery and Excitement need,
Their frail and fleeting smiles to feed.

Ah! "bonnie bird!"—thus ever rest,
Confiding in your love-built nest;
And when around you throng the few
I leave, who share my love with you,
Oh! warble soft, in friendship's ear,
  Her name, who'd gladly share your glec,
But do not sing *too sweetly*, dear,
  Lest you beguile them all from *me*.

VENUS AND THE MODERN BELLE.

Young Beauty look'd over her gems one night,
  And stole to her glass with a petulant air:
She braided her hair with their burning light,
  Till they play'd like the gleam of a glowworm
      there.

Then she folded, over her form of grace,
  A costly robe from an Indian loom,—
But a cloud overshadow'd her exquisite face,
  And Love's sunny dimple was hid in the gloom.

"It is useless!" she murmur'd,—"my jewels have lost
  All their lustre, since last they illumined my curls!"
And she snatch'd off the treasures, and haughtily toss'd,
  Into brilliant confusion, gold, rubies, and pearls.

Young Beauty was plainly provoked to a passion;
  "And what?" she exclaim'd, "shall the star of the ball
Be seen by the beaux, in a gown of this fashion?"—
  Away went the robe,—ribands, laces, and all!

"Oh! Paphian goddess!" she sigh'd in despair,
  "Could I borrow that mystic and magical zone,
Which Juno of old condescended to wear,
  And which lent her a witchery sweet as your own!"—

She said, and she started; for lo! in the glass,
  Beside her a shape of rich loveliness came!
She turn'd,—it was Venus herself! and the lass
  Stood blushing before her, in silence and shame.

"Fair girl!" said the goddess—"the girdle you seek
  Is one you can summon at once, if you will;
It will wake the soft dimple and bloom of your cheek,
  And, with peerless enchantment, your flashing
      eyes fill.

"No gem in your casket such lustre can lend,
  No silk wrought in silver, such beauty bestow;
With that talisman, heed not, tho' simply, my friend,
  Your robe and your ringlets unjewell'd may flow!"

"Oh, tell it me! give it me!"—Beauty exclaim'd,
  As Hope's happy smile to her rosy mouth stole:
"Nay! you wear it e'en now, since your temper is
      tamed,—
  'Tis the light of Good Humor,—that gem of the
      soul!"

THE FLOWER AND BROOK.

THE brook tripp'd by, with blossom and sigh,
And soft in music-murmurs sung,
While all the flowers that blossom'd nigh,
Were hush'd to hear that silver tongue.

"Ah, virgin violet!" breathed the brook,
"Whose blue eye shuns the light, the air,
I love you! in this true heart look,
And see—your own sweet image there!"

The bashful violet bent her brow,
But as she gazed, she sigh'd in sorrow,
"Oh! faithless heart—oh! idle vow!
Beloved to-day,—betray'd to-morrow!

"What see I, in that heart of thine?
There's not a flower that blooms above thee,
But there its image glows like mine,
Yet,—false and light! you say you love me!

"Go—changeful rover!—wander free,
With sunny glance, and voice beguiling,
And take my fondest sigh with thee,
To boast where other flowers are smiling!

"Go! tell the lily and the rose,
Of all the incense lavish'd o'er thee!
Go—wake *them* from their pure repose,
And bid them waste *their* blushes for thee!

"Go! breathe to them the music low,
Which all too oft beguiles the blossom!
But oh! *remember*, where you go,
My latest breath was on your bosom!"

THE STAR AND THE FLOWER;

OR, THE TWO PETS.

"Ad ogni uccello,
Suo nido è bello."

Ah . yours, with her light-waving hair,
That droops to her shoulders of snow,
And her cheek, where the palest and purest of roses
Most faintly and tenderly glow!

There is something celestial about her;
I never behold the fair child,
Without thinking she's pluming invisible wings
For a region more holy and mild.

There is so much of pure seraph-fire
Within the dark depths of her eye,
That I feel a resistless and earnest desire
To hold her for fear she should fly.

Her smile is as soft as a spirit's,—
  As sweet as a bird's is her tone ;
She is fair as the silvery star of the morn,
  When it gleams thro' the gray mist alone.

But mine is a simple wild-flower,
  A balmy and beautiful thing,
That glows with new love and delight every hour,
  Thro' the tears and the smiles of sweet spring !

Her eyes have the dark brilliant azure
  Of heaven in a clear summer night,
And each impulse of frolicsome, infantine joy,
  Brings a shy little dimple to light.

Her young soul looks bright from a brow
  Too fair for earth's sorrow and shame ;
Her graceful and glowing lip curls, even now,
  With a spirit no tyrant can tame.

Then let us no longer compare
  These tiny, pet-treasures of ours ;
For yours shall be loveliest still of the *stars*,
  And mine shall be fairest of *flowers*.

TO A FRIEND.

Oh, no! never deem her less worthy of love,
  That once she has trusted, and trusted in vain!
Could you turn from the timid and innocent dove,
  If it flew to your breast from a savage's chain?

She too is a dove, in her guileless affection,
  A child in confiding and worshipping truth;
Half broken in heart, she has flown for protection
  To you,—will you chill the sweet promise of youth?

To a being so fragile, affection is life!
  A rosebud, unbless'd by a smile from above,
When with bloom and with fragrance its bosom is rife—
  A bee without sweets—she must perish or love!

You have heard of those magical circles of flowers,
Which in places laid waste by the lightning are found;
Where they say that the fairies have charm'd the night hours,
With their luminous footsteps enriching the ground.

Believe me—the passion she cherish'd of yore,
That brought, like the storm-flash, at once on its wing
Destruction and splendor, like that hurried o'er,
And left in its track but the wild fairy-ring,—

All rife with fair blossoms of fancy and feeling,
And hope, that spring forth from the desolate gloom,
And whose breath in rich incense is softly up-stealing,
To brighten *your* pathway with beauty and bloom!

A TRIBUTE OF GRATITUDE.

"Know ye the land," where they welcome the stranger,
With *heart* as with hand, frank, confiding, sincere;—
Where the lonely, the languid, the sorrowing ranger,
Like a brother, they watch over, cherish, and cheer?

Where a smile warm and radiant everywhere meets him,
On earth,—in the air,—from the arch o'er his head,—
And the sweetest, and purest, and gayest, that greets him,
From the eyes of its own merry maidens, is shed?

"Know ye the land," in which nature is never
Without some wild blossom to twine in her hand?—

In the hearts of its children 'tis summer forever,—
The summer of love and joy :—" Know ye the land ?"

Where the gifted are met with a sympathy glowing
As that which a diamond yields to the light,
When it sends back the smile of the sunbeam, bestowing
New brilliance and bloom on the messenger bright ?

That land,—in the eyes, in the souls of whose daughters
Sleep all the rich glory and fire of its skies,
Subdued, as when far in the depth of the waters,
To Heaven its own soften'd image replies ?

There the bird, on whose bosom a rainbow is changing—
The Nonpareil—plays its soft plumage of blue ;
And Beauty,—as matchless,—'mid rare blossoms ranging,
Beams, blushes, and warbles,—a Nonpareil too !

There the Lory and Oriole glance on gay pinion,
There the regal Magnolia's snow-banners wave :—
'Tis the land of the high-hearted, proud Carolinian,
'Tis the land of the noble,—the bright, and the brave !

GARDEN GOSSIP,

Accounting for the coolness between the lily and violet.

" I WILL tell you a secret !" the honey-bee said,
To a violet drooping her dew-laden head ;
" The lily's in love ! for she listen'd last night,
While her sisters all slept in the holy moonlight,
To a zephyr that just had been rocking the rose,
Where, hidden, I hearken'd in seeming repose.

" I would not betray her to any but *you ;*
But the secret is safe with a spirit so true,
It will rest in your bosom in silence profound."
The violet bent her blue eye to the ground ;

A tear and a smile in her loving look lay,
While the light-wingéd gossip went whirring away.

" I will tell you a secret!" the honey-bee said,
And the young lily lifted her beautiful head;
" The violet thinks, with her timid blue eye,
To pass for a blossom enchantingly shy,
But for all her sweet manners, so modest and pure,
She gossips with every gay bird that sings to her.

" Now let me advise you, sweet flower! as a friend,
Oh! ne'er to such beings your confidence lend;
It grieves me to see one, all guileless like you,
Thus wronging a spirit so trustful and true:
But not for the world, love, my secret betray!"
And the little light gossip went buzzing away.

A blush in the lily's cheek trembled and fled;
" I'm sorry he told me," she tenderly said;
" If I mayn't trust the violet, pure as she seems,
I must fold in my own heart my beautiful dreams!"
Was the mischief well managed? Fair lady, is't true?
Did the light garden gossip take lessons of *you?*

DOUBTFUL VOWS.

A DUET.

" By the starlight of thine eye,
By thy soft cheek's changing dye,
By the dimple dancing out,
Peeping, playing round about,
'Mid the roses—like a sprite
In a garden of delight—"

" Vow not thou by radiant eyes,
Lo ! in tears their glory dies ;
Nor by youth's enchanting flower,
Roses die when summer's o'er ;
Nor by dimples that must hide
Soon as Sorrow comes to chide."

" By the graceful waving braid,
Half in light and half in shade,

Glittering gold or glossy brown,
From thy forehead floating down;
By the neck it makes more white
With its kisses soft and light—"

"Vow not thou by gleams of gold
Braided in a tress's fold;
Time will chase the light away,
Time will change the gold to gray;
Vow not thou by tints of snow,
Age will dim their virgin glow.

"Vow by something holier far
Than the charms of girlhood are;
Else, when rose and ray are fled,
And the ringlet's gloss is dead,—
Lost the dimple—dim the hue,
Thy light vows will alter too."—

"By the soul that fills thy face
With its own immortal grace,
Tuning glance, and step, and tone
Into music all its own,
Hallowing all thy grief and glee—
By thy *soul*, I love but thee!"

EARL ALBERT'S BIRD.

A SCOTCH SONG.

A GOWDEN cage Earl Albert had,
  A peerless bird he kept within it;
A bird o' beauty rare and glad,
  But 'twas na robin, finch, or linnet.

Earl Albert hung his cage wi' flowers,
  Wi' gems and silken gauds he deck'd it,
And siller locks upon the doors—
  "'Twould fly," said he, "I maun protect it!"

Earl Albert thought his bird was tame,
  Because its sang was saft an' tender,—
And Luti was its winsome name,
  And it was robed wi' jewell'd splendor.

The bonnie bird! its radiant eyes,
  Its tones o' luve sae wildly pleading,
The passer-by were more than wise
  Gin he could pass unharm'd—unheeding.

And unco weel he luved his pet,
  And mickle care he had to guard it,
For oh! its glancing eyes o' jet
  Still watch'd the door altho' he'd barr'd it.

"Ah! gin you luve me, let me go
  And I'll come back!" sae warbled Luti.
"Nay! cauld without the wind doth blow,
  Ye're safer in your cage, my beauty."

Just then a bairn cam tripping nigh,
  Wi' Iris wing and gowden quiver,
He waited till the earl went by,
  Then cried, "*I'll* settle that forever!"

Like lightning sped the sun-tipp'd shaft,
  The white breast heaved—the saft wings flut-
    ter'd,
While saucy Luve delighted laugh'd—
  "She'll soon break prison now," he mutter'd.

Earl Albert cam when morning shone,
New dainties for his darling bringing;
The door was wide! the bird was flown!
And thus afar he heard her singing—

"Oh! gin ye'd ruled by luve alane,
And gin ye'd left me free to fly, sir,
Save by yer leave I had na gane,
But *tyrants'* bars I break or die, sir!"

THE TALISMAN.

My darling child! beside my knee
She lingers, pleading low
For "just one more sweet fairy tale,
And then I'll let you go!"

"So listen, dear, and I will tell
How once to man was given,
An instrument so heavenly sweet
'Twas thought it *came* from Heaven.

" So daintily its strings were wrought,
So exquisitely fine,
A breath from Him who made, could break
The talisman divine.

" So prompt, too, with its eloquent tones,
This rare device they say,
That, without touch of human hands,
A wish could bid it play!

" In radiant Eden first 'twas heard,
Harmonious, mild, and clear;
And at the sound, each singing-bird
Its warble hush'd, to hear.

" From thence, with varying melody,
But never with a tone
So pure, so free, as then it had,
It pass'd from sire to son.

" And now, in murmurs soft and low
As rippling rills, it sang,
And now with wild, impassion'd flow,
Its clarion-music rang!

"If Love or Pity tuned the string,
  Or Memory ask'd its aid,
Sweet, pleading notes, the charmèd thing
  In tender cadence play'd.

"If Anger touch'd the quivering chords
  With trembling hand of fire,
What demon-tones—what burning words
  Resounded from the lyre!

"But oh! when soft Forgiveness came,
  And o'er the discord sigh'd,—
How like an angel's lute of love
  That fairy lyre replied!

"A fearful power the gift possess'd,
  A power for good or ill;—
Each passion of the human breast
  Could sweep the strings at will.

"And it could melt to softest tears,
  Or madden into crime,
The hearts that heard its thrilling strains,
  Wild, plaintive, or sublime.

" The oath within the murderer's heart,
Fair childhood's sinless prayer,
Hope's eager sigh, Affection's vow,
All found an echo there!

" What pity, that a gift so rich,
Attuned by love divine,
Was thus profaned by impious man,
At Guilt's unhallow'd shrine!"

Her eyes in innocent wonder raised,
As gravely still I spoke;
The child into my face had gazed,
But now the pause she broke :—

" Oh! were it mine, that wondrous toy,
That but *a wish* could wake!
Mamma, 'twould be my pride, my joy,
Soft melody to make!

" The evil spirits, tempting youth,
Should ne'er approach my treasure,
I'd keep it pure for Love, for Truth,
For Pity, Hope, and Pleasure!

"And they should play so blest a strain
Upon th' enchanted lyre,
That Heaven would claim it back again,
To join its own sweet choir."

"Keep, keep, my child, that promise still,
'The wondrous toy' is thine!
E'en now thy spirit tuned it;—'tis
"The human voice divine!

"Oh! ask of Heaven to teach thy tongue
A true, a reverent tone,—
Full oft attuned to praise and prayer,
And still to vice unknown!

"And rather be it mute for aye,
Than yield its music sweet
To Malice, Scorn, Impurity,
To Slander, or Deceit!

"Degrade not *thou* the instrument
That God has given to thee,
But, till its latest breath be spent,
Let Conscience keep the key!"

"LOVE WILL NOT STAY TO BE WEIGHED."

A SONG.

The maiden in doubt,
Said to Love with a pout,
"I shall weigh you with Wealth ere I take you!"
"Ah!" said Cupid, "take care!
Little Beauty, beware!
Lest Love should forever forsake you!"

She toss'd back her curls,
Braided lightly with pearls,—
"So saucy, young sir? I defy you!"
Then in one scale she roll'd
Half a million of gold,—
"Come hither, you rogue! let me try you!"

Love sigh'd and Love smiled,
Love's a singular child;
"Come, come now! jump in!" said the maid;

But she coax'd him in vain;
For he flew from her chain,
Singing—" Love will not stay to be weigh'd!"

Then, since my heart's offer
With Wealth's shining coffer
You balance,—remember, fair maid!
It were idle—'twere naught—
It were not worth a thought,
The love that would stay to be weigh'd!

ELLEN ARDELLE.

A SONG.

There were music and mirth in the lighted saloon;
The measure was merry,—our hearts were in tune,—
While hand link'd with hand in the graceful quadrille,
Bright joy crown'd the dance, like the sun on the rill,
And beam'd in the dark eyes of many a belle;
But the star of the ball-room was Ellen Ardelle!

She tripp'd with the grace of a wild forest fawn,
Her locks wore the soft amber glow of the dawn,
Her cheek, the rich flush of a sunset in May,
And pure—like the star-light—her eyes' azure ray;
Light, light as a feather her fairy foot fell;
Oh! vision of loveliness! Ellen Ardelle!

There are hundreds as brilliant, as graceful and fair;
But who, with so touching, so winning an air?
When softly she raises those eyes of deep blue,
What soul can resist them?—I cannot,—can you?
Ah! light heart! beware the bewildering spell
That lurks 'neath the lashes of Ellen Ardelle!

No jewel she needs, her young beauty to light;
Her glance would out-glow it, if ever so bright.
Her blush is all feeling,—her smile is all love;
She is tender and faithful, and pure as the dove;
But timid and wild, like a mountain gazelle,—
What fond hand shall tame her,—Young Ellen Ardelle?

ZULEIKA.

FROM THE SPANISH.

A LADY in a light caique,
  Abdallah's youngest daughter,
With Love's blush-rose upon her cheek,
  Look'd o'er the moonlit water.

Her snow-soft hand in Selim's lay,
  Her heart was wildly beating,
But still her dark eyes turn'd away
  To watch the shore retreating.

" Nay, look not there, my trembling dove!"
  Young Selim cried in sorrow,—
" My bride to-night, by Allah, love,
  I'll bear thee back to-morrow!"

"Too late!" the lady sigh'd, "oh! *now*,
If thou dost prize Zuleika,
Turn back!—point home thy shallop's prow,
Ere those forsaken seek her!

"When first my lips their light assent
To this light folly falter'd,
Love, only Love, his rainbow lent,
And still it smiles unalter'd.

"But oh! thro' tears of grief and shame
It glows; turn back, my bravest!
And blessings from Abdallah claim,
For her whose truth thou savest!"

Young Selim bent his lightning eyes
Back o'er the wild, blue water,—
With quivering lip he thus replies,
To old Abdallah's daughter:—

"Tis done, Zuleika! lo! we turn,
But never dream of Heaven
So fair to Moslem's eye did burn,
As that which thou hast riven!"

At fierce Abdallah's feet they knelt,
  And own'd the vows they'd plighted ;
His soften'd heart the story felt,
  His hand their hands united.

And long did Selim bless the hour
  That saw his Moorish beauty,
So meekly lay love's passion-flower
  Upon the shrine of duty!

LOVE AND LOGIC.

The gods one day sent Reason out,
  To look for Love,—their truant-boy!
They bade her seek him all about,
  And lure him home with tempting toy.

She found him in a rosebud rock'd,
  She begg'd him to be back in season ;
But still the boy the maiden mock'd,
  For—*Love will never list to Reason!*

The goddess held a jewel up,
  With Heaven's own glory flashing thro' it ;—
" Nay ! see my Rose's blushing cup !"
  Said Love,—" Your gem is nothing to it !"

" For shame ! false boy ! must *force* be tried ?
  Is't thus you waste this precious season ?"
" Take care ! d'ye know this bow ?" he cried !
  Ah ! *Love too oft has conquer'd Reason !*—

" I see your aim !—*your rhetoric* speeds
  On proud Olympus ill without me ;
But happy *Love* no *Reason* needs !
  Begone ! and when they ask about me,

" Just tell them, in my Rose's heart
  I've found so dear—so pure a treasure,
I grudge them not Minerva's art,
  Or laughing Hebe's cup of pleasure !"

The maid had not a word to say,—
  She knew the rogue was talking treason,—
But back to Ida bent her way ;
  For—*Love can better plead than Reason !*

TO LITTLE MAY VINCENT.

My wee-bit, bonny, blue-eyed May!
Well fits the name we gave in play;
For Spring, with all her tears and smiles,
Her frolic frowns and wooing wiles,
Is just like thee—so fresh, so bright,
With breath of balm and eyes of light.
My treasure, May! my nestling dove!
My wild-flower, nursed by Hope and Love!
My sunlit gem! my morning star!
Oh! there is nothing near or far,
Of soft or beautiful or free,
That does not mind my heart of thee.
Yet all combined,—star, blossom, bird,
  Bring to it no such joy divine,
As the first charily-utter'd word
  That falters from those lips of thine.

Twelve times the maiden-queen of night
Has donn'd her veil of silver light,
And walk'd the silent, heavenly plain,
Majestic 'mid her radiant train,
Since May first ope'd her playful eyes ;
And yet she is not over-wise ;
For even now she shouts with joy
  When on the floor the sunshine plays,
And deems the spot a golden toy,
  And creeps to lift its mocking rays.

Ah, May ! be still a child in this,
Through life, amid its gloom and bliss,
Though clouds of care be all about,
Those eyes will find the sunshine out,
Then pass the shade with Hope's delight,
And stop to play where Joy is bright.

A SONG.

Braid not the jewel,
  Love, in thy hair!
For such adornment
  Thou art too fair.

Suits not the diamond
  Tresses so light,
Floating like golden mist,
  Changefully bright.

Weave its wild lustre
  Thro' the dark braids,
Whose raven cluster
  Helen's eye shades!

There will its splendor
  Fittingly play;
Thou art too tender
  For such array.

Take this white rose, love,
  Stainless as thou,
Let it repose, love,
  By thy fair brow!

And as its fragrance
  Softly steals by,
Sweet as thy balmy breath,
  Pure as thy sigh,

Think of the lover,
  In whose fond sight,
No gem of Ophir
  Makes thee more bright!

"SHE LOVES HIM YET!"

A SONG.

SHE loves him yet!
I know by the blush that rises
Beneath the curls
That shadow her soul-lit cheek;
She loves him yet!
Thro' all Love's sweet disguises
In timid girls,
A blush will be sure to speak.

But deeper signs
Than the radiant blush of beauty,
The maiden finds,
Whenever his name is heard;—
Her young heart thrills,
Forgetting herself—her duty—
Her dark eye fills,
And her pulse with hope is stirr'd.

She loves him yet!
The flower the false one gave her
When last he came,
Is still with her wild tears wet.
She'll ne'er forget,
Howe'er his faith may waver,
Thro' grief and shame,
Believe it—she loves him yet!

His favorite songs
She will sing—she heeds—no other;
With all her wrongs
Her life on his love is set.
Oh! doubt no more!
She never can wed another:
Till life be o'er,
She loves—she will love him yet!

THE LILY'S REPLY.

The Rose-queen to a Lily said,—
"You bashful thing! hold up your head!
Since Heaven has lavish'd beauty, grace,
And fragrance, on your form and face,
Why waste it on the coarse dull earth?
Look up to Him who gave you birth.
See me! I lift my glowing cheek,
The holiest airs of heaven to seek.

"Free from my 'heart of heart' I give,
  (The Rose with Shakspeare held commune,)
Up to yon skies that bade me live,
  My incense, like a low-breathed tune.
Lily! look up! 'tis pleasant weather!
Let's brave this changing world together!"

The Lily to the Rose replied,—
"I dare not hold so lofty pride:

Befits in fair, as stormy weather,
That I and Meekness bend together;
For they who lift too high their heads,
When Heaven her sunshine o'er them sheds,
Too low beneath the tempest lie,
Forgetful of Love's sleepless eye.
And He who gave me sweetness—grace,
Bestow'd as well my fitting place;
And most I show my grateful care,
By yielding earth what I may spare;
And best to Him his gifts return,
By shedding round me, here below,
The wealth that fills my fragile urn;
He knows how true I thank Him so!"

"HAPPY AT HOME."

Let the gay and the idle go forth where they will,
In search of soft Pleasure, that syren of ill;
Let them seek her in Fashion's illuminèd saloon,
Where Melody mocks at the heart out of tune;

Where the laugh gushes light from the lips of the
maiden,
While her spirit, perchance, is with sorrow o'erla-
den;
And where, 'mid the garlands Joy only should braid,
Is Slander, the snake, *by its rattle* betray'd,
Ah! no! let the idle for happiness roam,
For me—I but ask to be happy at home!"

At home! oh, how thrillingly sweet is that word!
And by it what visions of beauty are stirr'd!
I ask not that Luxury curtain my room
With damask from India's exquisite loom;
The sunlight of heaven is precious to me,
And muslin will veil it if blazing too free;
The elegant trifles of Fashion and Wealth
I need not—I ask but for comfort and health!
With these and my dear ones—I care not to roam,
For, oh! I am happy, most "happy at home!"

One bright little room where the children may play,
Unfearful of spoiling the costly array;
Where he, too—our dearest of all on the earth,
May find the sweet welcome he loves at his hearth;

The fire blazing warmly—the sofa drawn nigh;
And the star-lamp alight on the table close by;
A few sunny pictures in simple frames shrined,
A few precious volumes—the wealth of the mind;
And here and there treasured some rare gem of art,
To kindle the fancy or soften the heart;
Thus richly surrounded, why, why should I roam?
Oh! am I not happy—most "happy at home?"

The little ones, weary of books and of play,
Nestle down on our bosoms—our Ellen and May!
And softly the simple, affectionate prayer,
Ascends in the gladness of innocence there;
And now ere they leave us, sweet kisses and light
They lavish, repeating their merry "good-night!"
While I with my needle, my book, or my pen,
Or in converse with *him*, am contented again,
And cry—"Can I ever be tempted to roam,
While blessings like these make me happy at home?"

HAPPINESS LOST AND FOUND.

OUR cot was in a forest glade,
Where sunbeams stole to mock the shade,
And wild-flowers round the lattice play'd,
By beam and breeze caress'd :
And in our Mary's form and face
Was all the blossom's glowing grace ;
A lovely human flower was she ;
Nay, more a bird in tireless glee,
The darling of the nest !
She came an orphan to our wild ;
But fondly on her kinsman's child
My mother her true welcome smiled,
And so our home was blest.

Yet I, alas ! unconscious then
How rich within our woodland glen

Were we, afar from world-worn men,
For gaudier pleasures pined:
For I had seen, in dreams at night,
A being lovely as the light,
With eyes like heaven, of changeful blue,
And hair that gleams of gold stole through,
And lips in dimples shrined.
Her name was Happiness, she said;
And soon by blind Ambition led,
I left our lowly love-warm'd shed,
To seek this maiden kind.

I sought her far—I sought her wide—
I sought her in the halls of pride;
Her angel smile was still denied,
Where gems less lovely shone.
I ask'd of Fame her fairest crown:—
With mocking laugh she cast it down.
No spell was in the wreath, tho' fair,
To win the maid with golden hair;
And I was all alone.
I ask'd of Wealth his coffers' key:
He smiled, and flung them wide to me,
The glittering treasure, far and free,
I lavish'd.—Soon 'twas flown.

It bought me rank ;—it bought me power ;—
It bought me Pleasure's fleeting flower,
And many a plaything of an hour :
    Ah, me ! 'twas little worth !
It could not buy that being fair,
The vision with the shining hair ;
No ! far from me her low sweet lay
Young Joy was warbling all the day,
    While I o'er half the earth
Went wandering for her looks of light.
At length I wearied of the sight
Of palace-halls. I dream'd one night
    Of her who gave me birth.

And coldly on the morrow-morn,
With sorrow in my soul and scorn,
I sought the glen where I was born,—
    How holy seem'd the air !
The wild-flower with its early glow
Still lightly laced the lattice low ;
Still sang the rill ;—the forest trees
Bent as of old beneath the breeze,
    And all was free and fair.
The Zephyr with its breath of balm,
The sunshine smiling soft and calm,

Wrought in my very heart a charm,
And made it Summer *there.*

Some dreamy moments pass'd before
My trembling hand unlatch'd the door,
And I beneath that roof once more
Stood silent with delight.
My mother welcomed back her boy ;
My bashful Mary blush'd her joy ;
And folding to my heart the prize
That now seem'd dearest in mine eyes,
And loveliest and most bright,
I saw again the vision fair,
The maiden with the radiant hair ;
For Joy and I had *parted there,*
As there we met that night !

Ah ! many a youth will search like me,
Will roam the land and cross the sea
In quest of Happiness, while she
Sits all the while unseen
Beside the very hearth he leaves,
And there her golden web she weaves,
Perchance array'd in lowly guise,

But still with heaven-illumined eyes,
    And frank and smiling mien.
We fondest prize the gem we miss ;
We pine for *absent* friendship's kiss ;
We know not, till we *lose*, the bliss
    That dwells at home serene.

KEEP, KEEP THE MAIDEN'S DOWRY.

A DISTINGUISHED NOBLEMAN REFUSED A DOWRY WITH HIS BRIDE—THE INCIDENT SUGGESTED THE FOLLOWING LINES.

Keep, keep the maiden's dowry,
    And give me but my bride,—
Not for her wealth I woo her,
    Not for her station's pride ;
She is a treasure in herself—
    Worth all the world beside.

Is not her mind a palace,
    Wherein are riches rare,

Bright thoughts that flash like jewels,
And golden fancies fair,
And glowing dreams of joy and hope,
That make sweet pictures there?

Keep, keep my lady's dowry,
Her hand, her heart I claim;
That little hand is more to me
Than power, rank, or fame;
That heart's pure love is wealth, my lord,
No more your coffers name!

No statue in your proud saloon
Can match her form of grace,
No gem that lights your casket
The radiance of her face.
In giving her, you give me all
I covet in earth's space.

Oh! make her mine, your idol child!
To be my prize and pride,
My star in every festival,
My trust should wo betide,
My bower's loveliest blossom,
Mine own, my worshipp'd bride.

THE LANGUAGE OF GEMS.

FAIR Flora of late has become such a blue,
  She has sent all her pretty dumb children to
    school;
And though strange it may seem, what I tell you is
    true,
  Already they've learn'd French and English by
    rule.

Bud, blossom, and leaf, have been gifted with speech,
  And eloquent lips breathing love in each tone,
Delighting such beautiful pupils to teach,
  Have lent them a language as sweet as their own.

No more is the nightingale's serenade heard ;
  For Flora exclaims, as she flies through her
    bowers,

"It is softer than warble of fairy or bird!
'Tis the music of *soul*—the sweet language of flowers!"

No longer the lover impassion'd bestows
The pearl or the ruby;—in Hope's sunny hours
He twines for his maiden a myrtle and rose—
'Tis the echo of Love, the pure language of flowers.

But the pearl and the ruby are sadly dismay'd;
I saw a fair girl lay them lightly aside,
And blushingly wreathe, in her hair's simple braid,
The white orange flower that betray'd her a bride;

And I fancied I heard the poor jewels bewail,
At least they *changed countenance* strangely, I'm sure;
For the pearl blush'd with shame, and the ruby turn'd pale:—
Indeed 'twas too much for a *stone* to endure.

And I, who had ever a passion for gems,
From the diamond's star-smile to the ruby's deep flame;

And who envy kings only their bright diadems,
  Resolved to defend them from undeserved shame.

What are jewels but flowers that never decay,
  With a glow and a glory unfading as fair ?
And why should not they speak their minds if they
      may ?
  There are " sermons in stones," as all sages de-
      clare.

And a wild " tongue of flame" wags in some of them
      too,
  That would talk if you'd let it—so listen awhile ;
They've a world of rich meaning in every bright
      hue—
  A ray of pure knowledge in each sunny smile.

Then turn to the blossoms that never decay :—
  Let the learned flowers talk to themselves on their
      stems,
Or prattle away with each other to-day ;—
  And listen with me to the Language of Gems.

The *Diamond* emblem of *Genius* would seem,
  In its glance, like the lightning, wild, fitful, divine—

Its point that can pierce, with a meteor-gleam,
Its myriad colors—its shadow and shine.

And more in that magic, so dazzling and strange;
Let it steal from Apollo but one sunny ray,
It will beam back a thousand that deepen and change,
Till you'd fancy a rainbow within it at play.

Fair Truth's azure eyes, that were lighted in heaven,
Have brought to the Sapphire their smile from above,
And the rich glowing ray of the Ruby is given,
To tell as it blushes of passionate Love.

The Chrysolite, clouded, and gloomy, and cold,
Its dye from the dark brow of Jealousy steals,
But bright in the Crystal's fair face we behold
The image of Candor that nothing conceals.

Young Hope, like the spring, in her mantle of green,
Comes robed in that color, soft, pleasant, and tender,
And lends to the Emerald light so serene,
That the eye never wearies of watching its splendor.

The rosy Cornelian resembles the flush
  That faintly illumines a beautiful face,
And well in its lovely and tremulous blush
  May Fancy the emblem of Modesty trace.

While Joy's golden smile in the Topaz is glowing,
  And Purity dwells in the delicate Pearl,
The Opal, each moment new semblances showing,
  May shine on the breast of some changeable girl.

Serene as the Turquoise, Content ever calm,
  In her pure heart reflects heaven's fairest hue bright,
While Beauty, exulting in youth's sunny charm,
  Beholds in the Beryl her image of light.

To the beaming Carbuncle, whose ray never dies,
  The rare gift of shining in darkness is given;
So Faith, with her fervent and shadowless eyes,
  Looks up, through Earth's night-time of trouble, to heaven.

There's a stone—the Asbestos—that, flung in the flame,
  Unsullied comes forth with a color more pure,—

11

Thus shall Virtue, the victim of sorrow and shame,
Refined by the trial, forever endure.

Resplendent in purple, the Amethyst sparkling,
On Pride's flowing garments may haughtily glow,
While Jet, the lone mourning-gem, shadow'd and darkling,
And full of sad eloquence, whispers of Wo.

But thousands are burning beneath the dark wave,
As stars through the tempest-cloud tremblingly smile,
Or wasting their wealth in some desolate cave,
And talking, perchance, like the rest all the while.

Then wreathe of the blossoms that never decay,
A chaplet, dear maiden, that fair brow above,
But within, wear their prototypes, purer than they,
Faith—Hope—Truth and Innocence—Modesty—Love.

And while in each jewel a lesson you see,
While one smiles approval—another condemns,
I'm sure you will listen, delighted with me,
To a language so true as the language of *Gems!*

THE LOVER'S LIST.

A BALLAD.

"Come, sit on this bank so shady,
  Sweet Evelyn, sit with me!
And count me your loves, fair lady!
  How many may they be?"

The maiden smiled on her lover,
  And traced with her dimpled hand,
Of names, a dozen and over,
  Down in the shining sand.

"And now," said Evelyn, rising,
  "Sir Knight! your own, if you please;
And if there be no disguising,
  The list will out-number these.

"Then count me them truly, rover!"
And the noble knight obey'd,
And of names, a dozen and over
He traced within the shade.

Fair Evelyn pouted proudly;
She sigh'd—"Will he never have done?"
And at last she murmur'd loudly,
"I thought he would write but *one!*"

"Now read!"—said the gay youth, rising—
"The scroll,—it is fair and free,
In truth there is no disguising,
That list is the world to me!"

She read it with joy and wonder,
For the first was her own sweet name,
And again and again written under,
It was still—it was still the same!

It began with—"my Evelyn fairest!"
It ended with—"Evelyn best!"
And epithets fondest and dearest
Were lavish'd between on the rest.—

There were tears in the eyes of the lady
 As she swept, with her delicate hand,
On the river-bank cool and shady,
 The list she had traced in the sand.

There were smiles on the lip of the maiden
 As she turn'd to her knight once more,
And the heart was with joy o'erladen,
 That was heavy with doubt before!

THE BIRTH OF THE CALLITRICHE;

OR, WATER-STAR.

> "Nothing in them, that doth range,
> But must suffer a sea-change
> Into something new and strange."—*Shakspeare.*

'Tis night—and the luminous depths of heaven
 With urns of fire are lit,
Each borne in a viewless spirit's hand,
 Who lightly floats with it.

And Dian—the queen of that graceful train,
  Sails by in her silver shell,
While softly rises the choral strain,
  With a rich and joyous swell.

Now, voice by voice they are dying away,
  Till all save one are still,
And that sings on with a cadence glad,
  Like the gush of a rippling rill.

It comes from one of the beauteous seven,
  The Pleiades pure and bright,
Who keep more fondly than all in heaven,
  Unstain'd their urns of light.

She sings, as she bends o'er her burning vase,
  And she sees in the wave below
Her beaming smile, and her form of grace,
  And her soft hair's golden flow.

But hark! a voice from the waters clear,
  And the Pleiad leans to listen,
With a glowing cheek and a charmèd ear,
  And eyes that tenderly glisten.

"Daughter of light!
  I pine, I pine,
By day and night,
  For thy smile divine!

"Oh! radiant maid,
  My dwelling share!
Our nymphs shall braid
  Thy shining hair.

"And I will keep
  Thy star-urn pure,
While thou shalt sleep
  In joy secure.

"Where stately stands
  My coral hall,
On golden sands
  Thy feet shall fall.

"From rosy shell
  Thy rosier lip,
Where dimples dwell,
  Shall nectar sip;

"And the tremulous play
  Of purest pearls,
With a pale soft ray
  Shall gem thy curls.

"Oh, the wave is fair
  And mild and blue,
As the azure air
  Thou wanderest through!

"Then, loveliest far
  Of Atlas' daughters,
Bless with thy star
  Our limpid waters!"

Wild and sweet was the lay of love,
  Upborne on the balmy air,
And the Pleiad stole from her bower above,
  To gaze in the waters fair.

Ah! fatal gaze! for so fondly smiled
  Those eyes from the stream below,
She plunged, and the lamp of her heavenly life
  Went out in its vase of snow.

But light to the element's edge sprang up,
  A starry shape in bloom,
A strange wild flower in a fairy cup,
  That shone in the water's gloom :

And they say the penitent Pleiad's tears
  Still feed that star of the wave,
As of old her smiles in holier spheres
  To the Urn their pure light gave.

A MAY-DAY SONG.

Yes ! thou shalt wear the wreath we are merrily braiding,
  Of buds and blooms—the beautiful roses of Spring !
Amid the hair, thy forehead of snow o'ershading,
  'Twill mock the blush that steals to thy cheek as we sing.

For thee we twine ;—for who could so gracefully
wear it
As she, whose heart is lovely and pure as the
rose ;
The wreath is thine, and the happiness each of us
share it,
For thou art so meek no envy can mar thy repose.

THE PARTING.

I LOOK'D not—I sigh'd not—I dared not betray
The wild storm of feeling that strove to have way,
For I knew that each sign of the sorrow *I* felt
Her soul to fresh pity and passion would melt,
And calm was my voice, and averted my eyes,
As I parted from all that in being I prize.

I pined but one moment that form to enfold,
Yet the hand that touch'd hers like the marble was
cold.—

I heard her voice falter a timid farewell,
Nor trembled, tho' soft on my spirit it fell,
And she knew not—she dream'd not the anguish of soul
Which only my pity for her could control.

It is over,—the loveliest dream of delight
That ever illumined a wanderer's night!
Yet one gleam of comfort will brighten my way,
Tho' mournful and desolate ever I stray:
It is this, that to her—to my idol, I spared
The pang, that her love could have soften'd and shared!

ASPIRATIONS.

I WASTE no more in idle dreams my life, my soul away;
I wake to know my better self,—I wake to watch and pray.

Thought, feeling, time, on idols vain, I've lavish'd all too long:
Henceforth to holier purposes I pledge myself, my song!

Oh! still within the inner veil, upon the spirit's shrine,
Still unprofaned by evil, burns the one pure spark divine
Which God has kindled in us all, and be it mine to tend
Henceforth with vestal thought and care, the light that lamp may lend.

I shut mine eyes in grief and shame upon the dreary past,
My heart, my soul pour'd recklessly on dreams that could not last.
My bark has drifted down the stream, at will of wind or wave,
An idle, light, and fragile thing, that few had cared to save.

Henceforth the tiller Truth shall hold, and steer as Conscience tells,
And I will brave the storms of Fate, tho' wild the ocean swells.

I know my soul is strong and high, if once I give it
sway;
I feel a glorious power within, tho' light I seem and
gay.

Oh! laggard soul! unclose thine eyes. No more
in luxury soft
Of joy ideal waste thyself! awake, and soar aloft!
Unfurl this hour those falcon wings which thou dost
fold too long;
Raise to the skies thy lightning gaze, and sing thy
loftiest song.

A SONG.

I TURN'D from the monitor,—smiled at the warning
That whisper'd of doubt—of desertion to me;
I heard of thy falsehood, the dark rumor scorning,
I gave up the soul of my soul unto thee!

Too wildly I worshipp'd thy mind-illumed beauty;
Too fondly I cherish'd my dream of thy truth;
Forgetting, in thee, both my pride and my duty,
I made thee the god of my passionate youth!

And dearly and deeply I rue that devotion,—
Thou hast broken the heart that beat only for thee!
Not even *thy* voice can now wake an emotion;
I am calm as thyself while I bid thee "be free!"

THE "FAIRER FLOWER."

"Oh! are they not most bright and fair?"
The youthful lady cried;
And pointed to her blossoms rare
With playful love and pride.

The soft moss-rose with veilèd bloom,
Droops o'er the hands that tie it;

The lily lends its light perfume,
  The woodbine clusters by it.

But on the lady's lovely face,
  A blush out-blooms the rose ;
And 'neath the hand that clasps the vase,
  Less fair the lily shows.

A soldier true and brave was he,
  And crown'd with loftiest honor ;
He bent his dark and dauntless eyes
  With soften'd gaze upon her—

" Dear lady, yes ! 'tis well the bower
  Its loveliest lends to thee,
But *I* can show a fairer flower
  If thou'lt but come with me !"

She gave her hand with artless grace,
  She cross'd the room half dreaming ;
And there he show'd her own sweet face
  Within the mirror beaming !

LENORE.

Oh! fragile and fair, as the delicate chalices,
  Wrought with so rare and so subtle a skill,
Bright relics, that tell of the pomp of those palaces,
  Venice—the sea-goddess—glories in still.

Whose exquisite texture, transparent and tender,
  A pure blush alone from the ruby *wine* takes;
Yet ah! if some false hand, profaning its splendor,
  Dares but to taint it with poison,—it breaks!

So when Love pour'd thro' thy pure heart his lightning,
  On thy pale cheek the soft rose-hues awoke,—
So when wild Passion, that timid heart frightening,
  Poison'd the treasure—it trembled and broke!

THE SOUL'S LAMENT FOR HOME.

As 'plains the home-sick ocean-shell
  Far from its own remember'd sea,
Repeating, like a fairy spell
  Of love, the charmèd melody
It learn'd within that whispering wave,
  Whose wondrous and mysterious tone
Still wildly haunts its winding cave
  Of pearl, with softest music-moan—

So asks my home-sick soul below,
  For something loved, yet undefined;
So mourns to mingle with the flow
  Of music, from the Eternal Mind;
So murmurs, with its child-like sigh,
  The melody it learn'd above,
To which no echo may reply,
  Save from thy voice, Celestial Love!

THE FLOWER AND THE HUMMING-BIRD.

Wild and light as a fawn in flight,
 With the glee and the grace of a playful child,
She tripp'd to the hill's unclouded height,
 And the dying day around her smiled.

Sunbeam and breeze were at play with her hair,
 (Where a few wild blossoms were braided low,)
Wooing it back from her shoulders fair,
 Lighting it up with a golden glow.

And lo! as we gazed on the beautiful girl
 With the joy that we ever from grace derive,
We saw something quiver thro' one soft curl,
 And struggle and gleam like a jewel alive!

What can it be? For a moment or two
 It burn'd with a brilliant ruby-ray,

The next, it shone with the sapphire's blue,
  And now with the amethyst's purple play!

What can it be? It is changing still
  To an emerald tint—to the sunshine's glow—
Can the maiden alter her gems at will?
  And gift with wings each luminous show?

With wings—they are fluttering, tiny, and light,
  Like those which we fancy the fairies wear—
Ah! look! the treasure has taken flight,
  'Twas a humming-bird caught in that golden
      snare!

Silly rover! you fly from those silken rings,
  Where Love—a light prisoner—*hugs* his chain!
Oh, you never will shut your shining wings
  On a flower so rare and sweet again!

THE SUITOR'S REPLY

TO THE MAIDEN WHO WISHED TO RETURN HIS GIFT.

Yes! I implore—upon my knee—
Return the costly gift to me!
Not that!—the gem, whose light I prize
Less than one smile from thy dear eyes!

You say 'tis all too rich and rare
For lowly maid like you to wear,
I've given you one more costly still—
Return me *that*, dear! Say you will!

Its lustre will outlast the star
That burns before us, pure and far,
Return me *that*—all gems above!
Yes, Margaret, yes! Return—my love!

TO —— ——.

THEY told me Beauty o'er thy face
  Had breathed her rarest, richest spell,
And lightly twined an airy grace
  In every curl that round it fell.

We met—and 'neath the veil of light
  And bloom that Beauty round thee flung,
I found a charm of holier might,
  For Love had tuned thy heaven-taught tongue.

'Tis said in Erin's sunny isle,
  That they who wear the shamrock leaf,
A blessing bring where'er they smile,
  That lights and warms the wildest grief.

Hast *thou* within thy bosom hid
  The charmèd flower from Erin's shore,
Which some fond fairy found amid
  Her blooming fields, and hither bore?

Ah, no! within those dark-blue eyes,
  Those graceful words, that winning smile,
A deeply sweet enchantment lies,
  Beyond the spell from Erin's isle!

Thou dost not need the charmèd flower,
  Thou dost not need the fairy's art;
In *feeling* dwells thy magic power,
  The leaf of love is in thy *heart*!

HYMN.

Approach not the altar
  With gloom in thy soul;
Nor let thy feet falter
  From terror's control!

God loves not the sadness
  Of fear and mistrust:
Oh serve Him with gladness—
  The Gentle, the Just!

His bounty is tender,
  His being is Love,—
His smile fills with splendor
  The blue arch above.

Confiding, believing,
  Oh! enter always
" His courts with thanksgiving—
  His portals with praise!"

Nor come to the temple
  With pride in thy mien;
But lowly and simple,
  In courage serene.

Bring meekly before Him
  The faith of a child:
Bow down and adore him,
  With heart undefiled;

And "by the still waters,"
  And through the green shade,
With Zion's glad daughters,
  Thy path shall be made!

TO ——.

THEY tell me I was false to thee,
But they are false who say it ;
The vow I made was pure and free,
And time shall ne'er betray it.

I laid my heart on virtue's shrine,
I loved truth, honor, kindness ;
I love them still, I thought them thine,
Too soon I wept my blindness.

'Tis *thou* wert false to them and me,
My worship still I cherish ;
My love, still true, has turn'd from thee,
To find them or to perish.

THE WORLD-WORN LYRE.

Love! no more, with soul of fire,
Sweep the strings and sound the lyre!
All too wild the sad refrain,
When thy touch awakes the strain.
Thou henceforth must veil thy face
With its blush of childish grace,
Still thy sweet entrancing tone,
Fold thy wings and weep alone.

Mirth! oh! ne'er again come thou
With thy careless, cloudless brow,
With thy frolic-fingers flying,
Lightly o'er the lyre replying,
Making music, like a smile,
Glisten thro' its strings the while.
Thou and I, gay sprite! must part,—
Go thou to some happier heart!

Lyre! amid whose chords my soul,
Lull'd, enchanted, proudly stole,

Folly, Vanity, and Mirth,
Long have tuned thy tones to earth,—
I will take thee, hush'd and holy,
Changed in heart, and sad and lowly,
Into Nature's mother-breast;
There I'll lay thee down to rest.

There her harmony shall blend
All its soul with thine, sweet friend!
Silent lie upon her shrine
Till some spirit more divine,
Mission'd from its home to thee,
Teach a holier melody;
Then, awaked by airs of heaven,
Be thy discord all forgiven!

Meekly let thy music low
With creation's chorus flow,
With the music of the spheres,
Into listening angels' ears!
Let, henceforth, thy sweetest lays
Be attuned to prayer and praise,
And naught earth-born e'er again
Thee, my pleading lyre, profane!

SONG.

I CANNOT forget him!
  I've lock'd up my soul;
But not till his image
  Deep, deep in it stole.

I cannot forget him!
  The Future can cast
No flower before me
  So sweet as the Past.

I turn to my books;
  But his voice rich and rare,
Is blent with the genius
  That speaks to me there.

I tune my wild lyre,
  But I think of the praise,
Too precious, too dear,
  Which he lent to my lays!

I cannot forget him!
  I try to be gay,
To quell the wild sorrow
  That rises alway;

But wilder and darker
  It swells, as I try;
If *Heaven* could forget him,
  So never can I!

I cannot forget him!
  I loved him too well!
His smile was endearment,
  His whisper a spell.

I fly from his presence;
  Alas! it is vain;
I see him—I hear him—
  He's with me again!

He haunts me forever;
  I worship him yet;
Oh! idle endeavor!
  I cannot forget!

THE EXILE'S LAMENT.

I AM not happy here, mother!
  I pine to go to you;
I weary for your voice and smile,
  Your love—the fond and true!

My English home is cold, mother,
  And dark and lonely too!
I never shall be happy here,—
  I pine to go to you!

Full many a simple melody
  I make of home and you;
But no one loves and sings the song
  As Lizzie used to do!

I've friends, who kindly welcome give,
  And whom I'll ne'er forget;
But they love others more than me,
  And I am not their pet!

In at my lattice laughs the sun,
  And plays about my feet;
I'd welcome it if you were here
  Its summer warmth to greet!

The sky ne'er seems so blue, mother,—
  So balmy soft the air!
And oh! the flowers are not so pure
  As those I used to wear!

My baby Ellen gaily plays,
  But none are here to note,
With partial praise, her winning ways,
  Or catch the gems that float—

The gems of thought that sparkle o'er
  Her mind's untroubled sea;
Then vanish in its depths before
  We well know what they be!

How oft, when lovelier than their wont
  Her cheeks' pure roses glow,
And fairer 'neath the sunlit hair
  Her veinèd temples show,

I want it watch'd by other eye,
  That face—so bright to me!
And sigh—"If mother now were by!"
  "If Lizzie could but see!"

Oh! my English home is cold, mother,
  And dark and lonely too!
I never shall be happy here,—
  I pine to go to you!

I will not call it "home," mother,
  From those I love so far!—
That only can be home to me,
  Where you and Lizzie are.

LEONOR.

Leonor loved a noble youth,
But light was Leonor's maiden truth;
She left her love for wealth forsooth.
  Faithless Leonor!

Now she paces a palace-hall;
Lords and ladies await her call,—
Wearily Leonor turns from all.
Haughty Leonor!

Leonor lies on a couch of down;
The jewel-light of a ducal crown
Gleams through her tresses of sunlit brown.
Beautiful Leonor!

Leonor's robe is a tissue of gold,
Flashing with splendor in every fold;
Bracelets of gems on her arms are roll'd.
Radiant Leonor!

Diamonds sparkle in Leonor's zone,
With a star-like glory in every stone;
But the heart they smile over is cold and lone.
Joyless Leonor!

To be free once more she would give them all,—
The crown, the couch, and the sculptured hall,
And the robe with its rich and shining fall.
Poor, poor Leonor!

Like a captive bird, through her cage's bar
Of gold, she looks on her home afar,
And it woos her there like a holy star.
Vainly, Leonor!

Leonor's lip has lost its bloom,
Her proud blue eyes are dark with gloom;
She will sleep in peace in her early tomb.
Lonely Leonor!

TO LIZZIE.

MINE own sweet sister, wheresoe'er I go
I hear thy voice melodiously low;
Thine eyes, thy soft, dark, eloquent, loving eyes,
Before me in remember'd beauty rise!

Doth nature robe her form in rich array,
Wreathing her brow with stars for jewels rare!
Zoning her waist with the green moss of May,
And broid'ring all her vest with blossoms fair?

Do her sweet tones—sweet as thine own the while,
  Forth from my home my willing feet allure,
To wander in the warm light of her smile,
  And bare my forehead to her breathing pure?

I sigh and think—if thou wert with me now,
  Exulting in thy youth, and health, and glee,
How wouldst thou toss the ringlets from thy brow,
  And join in all her joyous revelry!

How would thy heart's enthusiast pulses beat,
  Thy voice with all its wealth of music rise,
Her ever changing melody to meet,
  Love in thy soul, and rapture in thine eyes!

Oh! sweetest, loveliest! would that thou wert here,
  Heaven loses half her holy light to me;
Earth is ungraced with all her spring-tide gear,
  And life itself worth little without thee!

VICTORIA,

On her way to Guildhall.

THEY told me the diamond-tiar on her head
Gleam'd out like chain-lightning amid her soft hair,
They told me the many-hued glory it shed
Seem'd a rainbow still playing resplendently there ;
I mark'd not the gem's regal lustre the while,
I saw but her sunny, her soul-illumed smile.

They told me the plume floated over her face,
Like a snowy cloud shading the rose-light of morn :
I saw not the soft feather's tremulous grace,
I watch'd but the being by whom it was worn ;
I watch'd her white brow as benignly it bent,
While the million-voiced welcome the air around rent.

They told me the rich silken robe that she wore
Was of exquisite texture and loveliest die,
Embroider'd with blossoms of silver all o'er,
And clasp'd with pure jewels that dazzled the eye :
I saw not, I thought not of clasp, robe, or wreath,
I thought of the timid heart beating beneath.

I was born in a land where they bend not the knee,
Save to One—unto whom even monarchs bow down :
But lo ! as I gazed, in my breast springing free,
Love knelt to her sweetness, forgetting her crown ;
And my heart might have challenged the myriads there,
For the warmth of its praise, and the truth of its prayer.

And to her—to that maiden, young, innocent, gay,
With the wild-rose of childhood yet warm on her cheek,
And a spirit, scarce calm'd from its infantine play
Into woman's deep feeling, devoted and meek ;
To her—in the bloom of her shadowless youth—
Proud millions are turning with chivalrous truth.

It is right,—the All-judging hath order'd it so ;
 In the light of His favor the pure maiden stands :
And who, that has gazed on that cheek's modest glow,
 Would not yield without murmur his fate to her hands ?
Trust on, noble Britons ! trust freely the while !
I would stake my soul's hope on the truth of that smile !

NONE ARE POOR.

Alas ! for the gay, who in gorgeous array,
 And chariots of pride, to God's altars are roll'd :
They would turn from a love-breathing seraph away
 If he came not apparell'd in purple and gold !

She stood 'mid the splendid insignia of wealth ;
 But the jewels that shone o'er her beauty and bloom

Were less fair than the sunny ray, smiling by stealth
Through the rose-tinted damask that shaded the room!

In the flash of her glance there was passion and pride,
In the curve of her lip there was haughty contempt,
As she spoke of the power to riches allied,
Of the evil and pain from which she was exempt.

Another stood by, with a soul in her eye,
Out-glowing in lustre the sun-ray and gem;
And a fount in that soul of warm feeling and high,
Whose least emanation was worth all of them.

She had pass'd thro' the shadow and sunlight of life,
She had learn'd in its storms to exult and endure;
And her gentle reply with sweet wisdom was rife—
"To me, there are none in the universe—poor!"

FAZRY.

HER hands clasp'd in anguish—her black eyes bent low,
With motionless grace, as if sculptured in stone,
Half veil'd by her dark hair's magnificent flow,
Sweet Fazry is standing—a captive—alone!

"Kara Aly!"—the statue awakes to that name,
As the marble grew warm 'neath the love-spell of old!
Lo! her pale cheek is kindling with beautiful shame,
And her eye is on fire with emotion untold!

"Frail flower of Kazan! you were nursed, from your birth,
Amid luxuries rarest and richest of earth;—
Why left you that home, with the fierce mountain-chief?"
"I loved him!" she murmur'd, in passionate grief.

"So young and so lovely, a cavern your home!
Ne'er languish'd that spirit for freedom to roam?
Rude dwelling for creature so fragile and fair!"
"Ah, no!" she replied—"Kara Aly was there!"

MAY-DAY IN NEW ENGLAND.

Can this be May? Can this be May?
We have not found a flower to-day!
We roam'd the wood—we climb'd the hill—
We rested by the rushing rill—
And lest they had forgot the day,
We told them it was May, dear May!
We call'd the sweet wild blooms by name—
We shouted, and no answer came!
From smiling field, or solemn hill—
From rugged rock, or rushing rill—
We only bade the pretty pets
Just breathe from out their hiding-places;

We told the little light coquettes
  They needn't show their bashful faces,—
" One sigh," we said, " one fragrant sigh,
We'll soon discover where you lie!"
The roguish things were still as death—
They wouldn't even breathe a breath.
Alas! there's none so deaf, I fear,
As those who do not choose to hear!

We wander'd to an open place,
  And sought the sunny buttercup,—
That, so delighted, in your face
  Just like a pleasant smile looks up.
We peep'd into a shady spot
To find the blue " Forget-me-not!"
At last a far-off voice we heard,
  A voice as of a fountain-fall,
That softer than a singing-bird,
  Did answer to our merry call!
So wildly sweet the breezes brought
  That tone in every pause of ours,
That we, delighted, fondly thought
  It must be talking of the flowers!
We knew the violets loved to hide
The cool and lulling wave beside:—

With song, and laugh, and bounding feet,
  And wild hair wandering on the wind,
We swift pursued the murmurs sweet;
  But not a blossom could we find;—
The cowslip, crocus, columbine,
The violet, and the snow-drop fine,
The orchis 'neath the hawthorn-tree,
The blue-bell, and anemone,
The wild-rose, eglantine, and daisy,
Where are they all?—they must be lazy!
Perhaps they're playing "Hide and seek"—
Oh, naughty flowers! why don't you speak?
We have not found a flower to-day,—
They surely cannot know 'tis May!

You have not found a flower to-day!—
What's that upon your cheek, I pray?
A blossom pure, and sweet, and wild,
  And worth all Nature's blooming wealth
Not all in vain your search, my child!—
  You've found at least the rose of health!
The golden buttercup, you say,
That like a smile illumes the way,
Is nowhere to be seen to-day.
Fair child! upon that beaming face

A softer, lovelier smile I trace;
A treasure, as the sunshine bright,—
A glow of love and wild delight!
Then pine no more for Nature's toy—
You've found at least the flower of joy.
Yes! in a heart so young and gay,
And kind as yours, 'tis always May!
For gentle feelings, love, are flowers
That bloom thro' life's most clouded hours!
Ah! cherish them, my happy child,
And check the weeds that wander wild;
And while their stainless wealth is given,
In incense sweet, to earth and heaven,
No longer will you need to say—
"Can this be May? Can this be May?"

VIRGINIA.

I SAW her first—a petted child,
  Her eyes were blue as heaven;
Her cheek was dimpled when she smiled,
  Her lips a rose-bud riven.

Her form, the prettiest in the world,
  Her step—a fairy's flight,
Her hair, like clouded sunshine, curl'd
  In clusters wild and bright.

"A child," I said,—so artless, wild,
  And full of mirth her mien;
You'd deem her but a lovely child,
  Though she was just fifteen.

I met her on her way to school,
  The snow fell swift and still;
The morn was clear and bright, but cool,
  And I had felt the chill.

But idly at that childlike form
  Fierce Winter flung his dart;
Her frolic feet had kept her warm,
  And Love was at her heart.

Her small straw bonnet backward flung,
  Her cloak blown here and there,
While drops of snow-like jewels hung
  In her disorder'd hair.—

That dimpled cheek was flush'd and bright,
  A smile was on her lip;
Her eyes were full of wild delight,
  And gay her graceful trip.

She seem'd a sunbeam in my way,
  The vision warm'd my heart,
And Memory kept the blessèd ray
  Long after we did part.

Years went—again her path I've cross'd;
  Ah! from that form and face
What depth of bloom and light are lost,
  What wealth of artless grace!

The world has won her—she has learn'd
Its measured smile and tread ;
The foot that once the snow-flake spurn'd,
By courtly rule is led.

And Fashion's hand has smooth'd the fold
Of that luxuriant hair,
Where once the tress of glossy gold
Waved wildly on the air.

Yet oft, unbidden, to her eyes
Quick tears of Feeling start,
And while those gems of truth arise,
She's still a child at heart.

Alas ! in all her Beauty's power,
Proud, stately, and serene ;
She knows not one bright thrilling hour
Like those of gay fifteen !

TO ANNA,

In reply to a Letter.

Don't say you are "ugly," you darling!
  While still your sweet letters unfold
The same glowing soul that enliven'd
  Those delicate features of old!—

That soul, whose pure fire would illume, love,
  A cheek of less exquisite mould,
With a changeable beauty and bloom, love,
  To which Aphroditè's were cold.

Don't say you've grown "ugly and stupid,"
  While still in each line I can trace
Some glimpse of those lovely emotions
  Which once I could read in your face!

When you tell me your mind wears a chain, love,
When you tell me your heart is asleep,
Then may-be, but never till then, love,
The wreck of your beauty I'll weep.

WHAT I LOVE.

I DEARLY love a changing cheek,
That glows or pales as feeling chooses,
And lets the free heart frankly speak
Upon it what the tongue refuses.

Where eloquent blushes burn and fade,
Rich with the wealth of warm emotion;
Or starry dimples mock the shade,
Like jewels in a restless ocean.

I dearly love a speaking eye,
That tells you there's a soul to wake it;
Now fired with fancies wild and high,
Now soft as sympathy can make it.

An eye whose dreamy depths and dark,
  In Passion's storm can proudly lighten!
But where Love's tears can quench the spark,
  And Peace the sky serenely brighten!

I love a lip that eye to match,
  Now curl'd with scorn, now press'd in sadness,
And quick each feeling's change to catch,
  Next moment arch'd with smiles of gladness.

I love a hand that meets mine own
  With grasp that causes some sensation;
I love a voice whose varying tone
  From Truth has learn'd its modulation.

And who can boast that regal eye?
  That smile and tone, untaught by art?
That cheek of ever-changing dye?
  That brave, free, generous, cordial heart?

I need not name her! None who've heard
  Her welcome true—her parting blessing—
Her laugh, by lightest trifle stirr'd—
  Her frank reply—will fail in guessing!

ON A LANDSCAPE BY DOUGHTY,

Called "The Indian Summer."

Ah, yes! in the mist, whose soft splendor
 Is shed like a smile o'er the scene,
So rich, yet so meltingly tender,
 So radiant, yet so serene,—

In the azure air veiling the mountain,
 Far off, with its own robe of light,
In the gleam and the foam of the fountain,
 In the foliage so gorgeously bright,—

I see a wild beauty belonging
 To one sunny region alone—
New England, belovèd New England!
 The soul-waking scene is thine own!

And gazing entranced on the picture,
  Mine eyes are with tears running o'er;
For my heart has flown home to those mountains,
  And I am an exile no more!

Again through the woodlands I wander,
  Where autumn trees, lofty and bold,
Are stealing from bright clouds above them
  Their wealth of deep crimson and gold.

Where Nature is sceptred and crown'd,
  As a queen in her worshipping land;
While her rock-pillar'd palaces round,
  All matchless in majesty stand!

Where the star of her forest dominions,
  The humming-bird, darts to its food,
Like a gem or a blossom on pinions,
  Whose glory illumines the wood.

Where her loftiest, loveliest flower,*
  Pours forth its impassion'd perfume;
And her torrents, all regal in power,
  Are wreath'd with the sun-circle's bloom.

* The Magnolia.

Where, on cloud-pillows soft but resplendent,
  Our day-spirit floats to his rest;
And the moon, like a pure jewel-pendent,
  Is hung on night's love-breathing breast.

New England! belovèd New England!
  I breathe thy rich air as of yore;
For my heart is at home in those mountains,
  And I am an exile no more!

Yet not for thy beauty or glory,
  Though lofty and lovely thou art,
And not for thy proud haunts of story,
  These tears of deep tenderness start;—

There's a home in the heart of New England,
  Where once I was fondly caress'd!
Where strangers ne'er look'd on me coldly,
  And care never came to my breast!

Though warm hearts have cherish'd the exile
  In moments of sorrow and pain,
There's a home in the heart of New England,—
  Oh! when shall I see it again!

YOUR HEART IS A MUSIC-BOX, DEAREST!

A LOVE SONG.

Your heart is a music-box, dearest!
  With exquisite tunes at command,
Of melody sweetest and clearest,
  If tried by a delicate hand;
But its workmanship, love, is so fine,
  At a single rude touch it would break;
Then oh! be the magic key mine,
  Its fairy-like whispers to wake!
And there's one little tune it can play,
  That I fancy all others above—
You learn'd it of Cupid one day—
  It begins with and ends with "I love!"
      "I love!"
  My heart echoes to it "I love!"

THE CHERUB'S SECRET.

WHAT made my Ellen start and smile,
  Then sink in soft repose again,
As if some joyous thought the while
  Had darted through her slumbering brain,
Like rosy lightning brief and bright,
Illumining a summer night?

Perhaps a viewless cherub stole,
  Young as thyself, as pure and fair,
On tiny pinions to thy soul,
  And whisp'ring some sweet secret there,
Awoke that smile of heavenly glee:
My Ellen! wake—and tell it me!

HYMN TO THE VIRGIN.

Mother of the spirit-child!
Of the guileless and the meek
Mournful are thine eyes, but mild
With a beauty from above;
Pale, but eloquent with love,
Thy youthful brow and cheek!
Thou, oh! thou hast known a parent's wasting grief!
A suppliant parent kneels, imploring thy relief!

By the pure and solemn joy
Filling all thy maiden breast,
When the precious heaven-born boy,
Glowing with celestial charms,
Lay within those virgin arms
A bright and wondrous guest!
Hear, in mercy, hear the faltering voice of grief!
A suppliant mother kneels, imploring thy relief!

By thine anguish in that hour,
Hour of wo and dread, when Death
Dared to stay the awful power,
High, majestic, yet benign;
Dared to seal the truths divine
Which dwelt upon his breath!
By thy hope, thy trust, thy rapture, and thy grief,
Oh! sainted Marie! send this breaking heart relief!

THE DYING ROSE-BUD'S LAMENT.

Ah me! ah! wo is me!
That I should perish now,
With the dear sunlight just let in
Upon my balmy brow!

My leaves, instinct with glowing life,
Were quivering to unclose!
My happy heart with love was rife!
I was almost a Rose!

Nerved by a hope, warm, rich, intense,
  Already I had risen
Above my cage's curving fence,
  My green and graceful prison!

My pouting lips, by Zephyr press'd,
  Were just prepared to part,
And whisper to the wooing wind
  The rapture of my heart!

In new-born fancies revelling,
  My mossy cell half riven,
Each thrilling leaflet seem'd a wing
  To bear me into heaven.

How oft, while yet an infant flower,
  My crimson cheek I've laid
Against the green bars of my bower,
  Impatient of the shade!

And pressing up and peeping through
  Its small but precious vistas,
Sigh'd for the lovely light and dew
  That bless'd my elder sisters!

I saw the sweet breeze rippling o'er
   Their leaves that loved the play,
Though the light thief stole all their store
   Of dew-drop gems away.

I thought how happy I should be
   Such diamond wreaths to wear,
And frolic with a rose's glee,
   With sunbeam, bird, and air!

Ah me! ah! wo is me! that I,
   Ere yet my leaves unclose,
With all my wealth of sweets must die
   Before I am a Rose!

THE UNEXPECTED DECLARATION.

"Azure-eyed Eloise! beauty is thine,
Passion kneels to thee, and calls thee divine;
Minstrels awaken the lute with thy name;
Poets have gladden'd the world with thy fame;

Painters, half holy, thy loved image keep;
Beautiful Eloise! why do you weep?"

Still bows the lady her light tresses low,—
Fast the warm tears from her veilèd eyes flow!

"Sunny-hair'd Eloise! wealth is thine own;
Rich is thy silken robe—bright is thy zone;
Proudly the jewel illumines thy way;
Clear rubies rival thy ruddy lip's play;
Diamonds like star-drops thy silken braids deck;
Pearls waste their snow on thy lovelier neck;
Luxury softens thy pillow for sleep—
Angels watch over it!—Why do you weep?"

Bows the fair lady her light tresses low,—
Faster the tears from her veilèd eyes flow!

"Gifted and worshipp'd one! Genius and Grace
Play in each motion, and beam in thy face:
When from thy rosy lip rises the song,
Hearts that adore thee the echo prolong!
Ne'er in the festival shone an eye brighter,
Ne'er in the mazy dance fell a foot lighter.

One only spirit thou'st fail'd to bring down,—
Exquisite Eloise! why do you frown?"

Swift o'er her forehead a dark shadow stole,
Sent from the tempest of pride in her soul!

"Touch'd by thy sweetness—in love with thy
grace—
Charm'd by the magic of mind in thy face—
Bewitch'd by thy beauty—e'en his haughty strength—
The strength of the stoic, is conquer'd at length!
Lo! at thy feet—see him kneeling the while—
Eloise! Eloise! why do you smile?"

The hand was withdrawn from her happy blue eyes,
She gazed on her lover with laughing surprise;
While the dimple and blush, stealing soft to her cheek,
Told the tale that her tongue was too timid to speak!

WHAT CAN BE THE MATTER WITH LIZZIE?

WHAT can be the matter with Lizzie to-night?
Her eyes, that in tears were so touchingly tender,
For twenty-four hours have been filling with light,
Till I scarcely dare meet their bewildering splendor.

You'd almost imagine a star had been lighted
Within her—a new-born and beautiful flame,
To bless with its pure ray her spirit benighted,
And smile thro' those eyes to which sorrow's cloud came.

What can be the matter with Lizzie!—her cheek,
That of late has been dimpleless, colorless, cold,
Has gather'd a glow and a glory, that speak
Like an eloquent voice of a rapture untold.

What can be the matter with Lizzie!—her tone,
That was doubting and faint in its low melody

As the morning ray rising thro' mist-tears alone,
Or the sound of a bell ringing soft in the sea,—

Has suddenly thrill'd to a richness and fervor,
A passionate sweetness, untroubled and deep—
You would think in her heart had arisen to nerve her,
An angel,—awaken'd from sorrow and sleep.

It is Love! it is Love! by the joy that is stealing
Like light o'er her forehead I know it is Love!—
He has touch'd with his wand the wild fountain of feeling,
He floats like a spirit that fountain above.

He has kindled his star-lamp—the deathless—the pure—
Within—and her heart's hidden riches are shown;
His own seraph voice has breathed melody to her—
And hers has caught all its deep magic of tone.

Oh! still may that voice keep its sweetness and joy,
And still may that cheek wear its glow of delight,
And those dear eyes, unshadow'd by sorrow's alloy,
Still beam with the fondness that fills them to-night.

MINA DOLCE.

A SONG.

Beneath Italia's laughing skies,
When joy the summer hour beguiled;
I found one day a lovely prize,
A blossom bright and wild.
Ah! Mina Dolce! Cara Mina! graceful Rose of Italie!
Dost thou bloom there in thy beauty still,—and is thy bloom for me?

I raised its tender cheek to mine,
I woke it from its pure repose;
I kiss'd away its dew divine!
Its tears!—my radiant Rose!
Ah! Mina Dolce! Cara Mina! blushing flower of Italie!
Art thou smiling in thy bower still,—and is thy smile for me?

I've gazed since then on loftier flowers,
In scenes more richly, grandly wild,
Ne'er found I bloom in Northern bowers
To match Italia's child.
Ah! Mina Dolce! Cara Mina! virgin Rose of Italie!
May I wear thee on my heart, and wilt thou give thy tears to me?

LINES

Suggested by a mourning-locket, in which was painted a winged Cherub, with the motto—"Je veille sur toi, ma mère!"

Je veille sur toi, ma mère!
I hear thy softest sigh of love,
I listen to thy lightest prayer,
And echo it above.

I see thee when, in lonely hour,
  My semblance wins thy ready tear;
Thou canst not hear my spirit step,
  But, mother! I am near!

When glowing morn the mountain treads
  With foot of fire and dewy eye,
And dazzled seraphs veil their heads
  Before the light on high!

And when beneath my home of joy
  The stars are smiling through the air,
Where angels roam on blest employ,
  Je veille sur toi, ma mère!

While o'er thy wearied frame is shed
  The welcome balm of soothing sleep,
Lightly o'er that belovèd head—
  My vigils still I keep!

Dost thou not see in visions fair,
  A radiant being wander by?
And hear a soft voice murmuring there,
  "My mother! it is I?"

And when above my early grave
  Thy gentle spirit prays relief,
Feel'st thou no angel-plumage wave
  Above thee in thy grief?

Je veille sur toi, ma mère!
  Oh! still thy lost but happy boy
Is near thee, with thee everywhere,
  In sorrow and in joy.

Forget not then, where'er thou art,
  The promise-words that bless thy prayer,
But wear them in thy "heart of heart,"
  "Je veille sur toi, ma mère!"

WHY WILL A ROSE-BUD BLOW?

I WISH the bud would never blow,
'Tis prettier and purer so;
It blushes through its bower of green,
And peeps above the mossy screen

So timidly, I cannot bear
To have it open to the air.
I kiss'd it o'er and o'er again,
As if my kisses were a chain,
To close the quivering leaflets fast,
And make for once—a rose-bud last!
But kisses are but feeble links
For changeful things, like flowers, methinks;
The wayward rose-leaves, one by one,
Uncurl'd and look'd up to the sun,
With their sweet flushes fainter growing,
I could not keep my bud from blowing!
Ah! there upon my hand it lay,
And faded, faded fast away;
You might have thought you heard it sighing,
It look'd so mournfully in dying.
I wish it were a rose-bud now,
  I wish 'twere only hiding yet,
With timid grace its blushing brow,
  Behind the green that shelter'd it.
I had not written were it so,
Why would the silly rose-bud blow?

FANNY'S ERROR.

FANNY shuts her smiling eyes,
Then, because she cannot see,—
Thoughtless simpleton! she cries,
"Ah! you can't see me!"

Fanny's like the sinner vain,
Who with spirit shut and dim,
Thinks because he sees not Heaven,
Heaven cannot see him!

NEW ENGLAND'S MOUNTAIN-CHILD.

WHERE foams the fall—a tameless storm—
Through Nature's wild and rich arcade,
Which forest-trees entwining form,
There trips the Mountain-maid!

She binds not her luxuriant hair
  With dazzling gem or costly plume,
But gayly wreathes a rose-bud there,
  To match her maiden-bloom.

She clasps no golden zone of pride
  Her fair and simple robe around ;
By flowing riband, lightly tied,
  Its graceful folds are bound.

And thus attired,—a sportive thing,
  Pure, loving, guileless, bright, and wild,—
Proud Fashion ! match me in your ring,
  New England's Mountain-child !

She scorns to sell her rich, warm heart,
  For paltry gold, or haughty rank,—
But gives her love, untaught by art,
  Confiding, free, and frank !

And once bestow'd,—no fortune-change
  That high and generous faith can alter ;
Through grief and pain—too pure to range—
  She will not fly or falter.

Her foot will bound as light and free
  In lowly hut as palace-hall;
Her sunny smile as warm will be,—
  For Love to her is all!

Hast seen where in our woodland-gloom
  The rich Magnolia proudly smiled?—
So brightly doth she bud and bloom,
  New England's Mountain-child!

THE BABY AND THE BREEZE.

The breeze was high, and blew her sun-brown tresses
  About her snowy brow and violet eyes;
  And she—my Ellen—brave and sweetly wise,
In gay defiance of its rough caresses,
With rosy, pouting mouth, essay'd at length
To blow the rude airs back, that mock'd her baby-strength.

Ah! thus when Fortune's storms assail thy soul,
Yield not, nor shrink! but bear thee bravely still
Against their fury! With thine own sweet will
And childlike faith, oppose their fierce control,
So shalt thou bloom at last, my treasured flower,
Unharm'd by tempest-shock, in Heaven's calm summer bower!

LINES

ON HOWARD'S PICTURE OF "THE HOURS AWAKING THE MORNING."

She sleeps! on her cloud-pillows softly reclining,
Her glowing cheek dimples with dreamy delight,
Around her white shoulders rich sun-tresses twining,
With dim, dewy lustre, illumine the night;—

Yes! faint through the mist that enwreathes her reposing,
The gleam of that golden hair glistens the while,

Making twilight on high;—till those blue eyes, unclosing,
  Shall flash on creation the wea.th of their smile!

She sleeps! and the stars have gone by in their glory,
  Nor woke with their wing'd feet the dreamer they met!
And Dian has stolen to tell the love-story
  Her blooming Endymion listens to yet!

She sleeps! the young goddess Aurora!—so glowing,
  So sweet are her visions, she will not awake!
And silent and swift are the dim Hours going,—
  But hark! o'er the stillness what music doth break!

Behold! through the mist, the fair Hour of the Morning,
  With smiles of arch meaning, floats gracefully by;
Her finger uplifted in frolicsome warning,
  With song on her lip, and reproof in her eye!

"Sweet sluggard! awaken!—Apollo is near!
Oh! fly ere the god shall thy slumbers surprise!
His flame-wingèd coursers already I hear!
Aurora! my sister!—awaken! arise!"

And the goddess springs up from the slumbers that bound her,
And pauses in blushing bewilderment there;
Her rosy smiles melting the mist-wreath around her,—
Her gold-tresses shedding soft dew on the air!

Now slowly she comes!—Heaven kindles before her,—
Her lark warbles proudly his passionate lay,—
Earth woos with a smile the light step of Aurora,—
And Beauty and Music awake in her way!

THE CHILD PLAYING WITH A WATCH.

Art thou playing with Time in thy sweet baby-
glee ?
Will he pause on his pinions to frolic with thee ?
Oh ! show him those shadowless, innocent eyes,
That smile of bewilder'd and beaming surprise ;
Let him look on that cheek where thy rich hair re-
poses,
Where dimples are playing "bopeep" with the roses ;
His wrinkled brow press with light kisses and warm,
And clasp his rough neck with thy soft wreathing
arm.
Perhaps thy bewitching and infantine sweetness
May win him, for once, to delay in his fleetness ;
To pause, ere he rifle, relentless in flight,
A blossom so glowing of bloom and of light.
Then, then would I keep thee, my beautiful child,
With thy blue eyes unshadow'd, thy blush undefiled ;

With thy innocence only to guard thee from ill,
In life's sunny dawning, a lily-bud still!
Laugh on! my own Ellen! that voice, which to me
Gives a warning so solemn, makes music for thee;
And while I at those sounds feel the idler's annoy,
Thou hear'st but the tick of the pretty gold toy;
Thou seest but a smile on the brow of the churl,
May his frown never awe thee, my own baby-girl.
And oh! may his step, as he wanders with thee,
Light and soft as thine own little fairy-tread be!
While still in all seasons, in storms and fair weather,
May Time and my Ellen be playmates together.

WHY DON'T HE COME?

All the girls in the village save me have gone forth,
To meet the brave soldiers return'd from the North,
They have donn'd the best kirtle and braided their hair,
And gayly their voices ring back on the air;

But I am too happy to care for my dress,
Or to bind with bright ribands the wild-waving tress,
For the fairest, and bravest, and best of the band,
Will claim, ere the morrow, this heart and this hand.
Hush! hark! far away! 'tis the bugle and drum!
Now louder and nearer—oh! why don't he come?

I cannot go forth with the others to claim
His smile—his caresses—I cannot for shame!
For my love is too holy, my joy is too high,
To bear the light gaze of each villager's eye;
He would think I had changed,—I should shrink from his touch,—
I should hate them to see that I love him so much.
But here! oh! how fondly I'll welcome him home!
He knows I am waiting him—why don't he come?

Perhaps cousin Mabel has seen him ere this,—
She would not be bashful at claiming a kiss;
How exulting she look'd as she join'd the gay girls,
With those red berries wreathing her shadowy curls!
It is true all the lads say her smile is divine,
But I don't think her eyes are so pretty as mine;—
So black and so bold! and they dazzle one so!
My Willie loves blue eyes and light hair, I know:

He will not forget his own Ellen at home,
For Mabel or any one,—when will he come?

I'm weary of waiting—how strangely unkind
To linger so from me,—I've made up my mind
I won't kiss him now, when he does—ah! behold!
Who hastes o'er the common with bearing so bold?
He waves his plumed cap! it is he! it is he!
Bless his heart—how he flies now he's caught sight
of me!
Ah! Mabel may listen the bugle and drum,
And bewitch the whole regiment—Willie has come!

ON A PICTURE,

Representing a maiden with a pair of scales, and Love with a butterfly; the winged boy rises, as he should, and the motto beneath is—"Love is the lightest!"

Silly maiden, weigh them not!
Butterflies are earthly things;
Thou forget'st their lowly lot,
Gazing on their glittering wings.

Rather weigh thy taper pale
  With the light by Luna given ;
Will the heaven-ray turn the scale ?
  Will the earth-lamp rise to heaven ?

Love,—ethereal, holy Love !
  Buoyant, joyous, proud, and free,
Maiden, see ! he soars above
  Worldly Pride and Vanity !

Rightly to its native earth
  Sinks the gilded insect-fly ;
Love—of holier, heavenlier birth—
  Rises tow'rds his home on high !

Maiden ! throw the scales away,
  Never weigh poor Love again ;
Let his pinions freely play,
  Bind him not with vassal-chain !

See ! he lifts his wondering eye
  Half reproachfully to thee ;—
Measured with a butterfly !
  I'd take wing if I were he !

If he must be proved and tried,
  Weigh him in thine own true heart,
'Gainst a frowning world beside,—
  Wealth and rank 'gainst bow and dart!

If he do not scorn the measure,
  Soaring high o'er them and thee,—
Worth the world and worldly treasure,—
  Mark me! Love outweighs the three!

ELLEN LEARNING TO WALK.

My beautiful trembler! how wildly she shrinks!
  And how wistful she looks while she lingers!
Papa is extremely uncivil, she thinks,—
  She but pleaded for one of his fingers!

What eloquent pleading! the hand reaching out,
  As if doubting so strange a refusal;
While her blue eyes say plainly, "What is he about
  That he does not assist me as usual?"

Come on, my pet Ellen! we won't let you slip,—
Unclasp those soft arms from his knee, love;
I see a faint smile round that exquisite lip,
A smile half reproach and half glee, love.

So! that's my brave baby! one foot falters forward,
Half doubtful the other steals by it!
What, shrinking again! why, you shy little coward!
'Twon't kill you to walk a bit!—try it!

There! steady, my darling! huzza! I have caught her!
I clasp her, caress'd and caressing!
And she hides her bright face, as if what we had taught her
Were something to blush for—the blessing!

Now back again! Bravo! that shout of delight,
How it thrills to the hearts that adore her!
Joy, joy for her mother! and blest be the night,
When her little light feet first upbore her!

ON PARTING FOR A TIME WITH AN INFANT'S PORTRAIT.

Fair image of my fairer child!
  Full many a moment's weary wo
By those blue eyes has been beguiled!
  How can I let my idol go?

For when my living treasure sleeps,
  And hides her bashful glance of glee,
Thy cherub face unchanging keeps
  Its precious bloom and smiles for me!

There still I see the flossy hair
  That bathes with light her glowing face;
Her dimpled hands so round and fair,—
  Her fragile form,—her childish grace!

Yet go! and with those earnest eyes,
  O'ershadow'd by thy silken curl,
Gaze smiling into stranger-hearts,
  And bid them bless my fairy girl!

LUCY'S GEM.

A TRUE STORY.

"You've read, my pet, in olden story,
  That oft o'er royal infant's bed,
Some mystic gift of grace or glory
  By fairy hands was shed.

"I know a child in modern days,
  Who, when a baby, thus was bless'd ;
But 'twas by One of rarer skill
  Than fays of old possess'd.

"This Being, kind as powerful, lent
  The child two wondrous living gems,
More precious than the costliest stone
  In Eastern diadems.

"And fair they shone from morn till night,
Those treasures, 'neath the lifted lid;
But when the gems of Heaven came out,
The gems of earth were hid;

"For oh! so delicately wrought,
So dainty, and so pure were they,
The lamp-light and the evening air
Would dim their azure ray.

"In each white case a magic well,
A little, fairy, charmèd thing,
At times, to bathe the jewels, pour'd
Its never-failing spring.

"But more amazing gifts than these,
Each tiny talisman possess'd;
Now was she not a favor'd child,
To be so richly bless'd?

"No sooner did she raise the lid,
Than suddenly, in each gem of light,
A perfect little picture came,
In colors pure and bright!"

"Mamma! and were they all her own?
And might she always with them play?
What color were the toys, mamma?
What kind of stones were they?"

"Two beaming sapphires! Heaven's own light
And color shone within them soft;
But clouds would o'er them flit at times,
And dew would dim them oft.

"Each in an ivory casket kept,
Whose lid was moved on viewless hinge,
With azure scroll-work all inlaid,
And trimm'd with silken fringe.

"Sometimes the child the caskets lock'd,
And kept them closed for many an hour;
And none could lift the little lids,
Save the kind Giver's power.

"But then, when He commanded her
To ope each tiny oval case,
The gems within, by some strange charm,
Had gain'd new light and grace.

" 'Twas painted with consummate art,
'Twas copied with a skill divine,
From whatsoever chanced, just then,
Before the gem to shine.

" Was it a friend's belovèd face?
Not Raphael's self the breathing form
With such celestial truth could trace,
So life-like, bright, and warm!

" Was it a landscape? lo! within
Her jewels waved the foliage green,—
Hill, river, cot, and cloud, were there,
And Heaven o'erarch'd the scene.

" All day, the great, good sun for them
New pictures of delight would weave,
'The crimson coming of the morn,
The funeral pomp of eve.'

" The tiniest flower that deck'd the bower,
Was imaged in each azure gem;
For them the rainbow smiled from heaven;
The stars came out for them!

"But oh! most wonderful of all!
These faithful friends to none betray'd
The shifting pageant, as it pass'd,
Save to the little maid.

"When others gazed, they only saw
A deep blue light, that softly smiled,
Untroubled, save at times by tears,
Shed o'er them by the child.

"Though deep within, e'en while they look'd,
The mimic diorama play'd,
The gazers could but guess at it,
It smiled but on the maid."

"Mamma! mamma! who was the child?"
"Her name, my love, was Lucy Grey."
"Why! that's *my* name! you *know*, mamma,
I've no such toys as they!"

"Indeed you have! This very hour,
There is a portrait in them drawn
Of one you love. Go now, my child,
And shut them till the dawn."

"Oh! sweet mamma! I've caught you now;
  You needn't try to look demure;
You've made a cunning story out;
  But I am right, I'm sure.

"*Yours* is the portrait painted there,
  In colors beautiful and bright;
I'll shut you up, and keep you in,
  To dream about! Good-night!"

"Stay, Lucy, love; you'll not forget,
  When you repeat your nightly prayer,
To thank the Giver of all good
  For gifts so rich, so fair?"

"No, dear mamma! and I will try
  To keep my spirit pure and true,
That so the costly gems He gave,
  Lose not their heavenly hue."

THE DAISY'S MISTAKE.

A SUNBEAM and zephyr were playing about,
One spring, ere a blossom had peep'd from the stem,
When they heard, underground, a faint, fairy-like shout;
'Twas the voice of a field-daisy calling to them.

"Oh! tell me, my friend, has the winter gone by?
Is it time to come up? Is the Crocus there yet?
I know you are sporting above, and I sigh
To be with you and kiss you;—'tis long since we met!

"I've been ready this great while,—all dress'd for the show;
I've a gem on my bosom that's pure as a star;

And the frill of my robe is as white as the snow ;
  And I mean to be brighter than Crocuses are."

Now the zephyr and sunbeam were wild with delight !
  It seem'd a whole age since they'd play'd with a flower ;
So they told a great fib to the poor little sprite,
  That was languishing down in her underground bower.

" Come out ! little darling ! as quick as you can !
  The Crocus, the Cowslip, and Buttercup too,
Have been up here this fortnight, we're having grand times,
  And all of them hourly asking for you !

" The Cowslip is crown'd with a topaz tiara ;
  The Crocus is flaunting in golden attire ;
But you, little pet ! are a thousand times fairer ;
  To see you but once, is to love and admire !

" The skies smile benignantly all the day long ;
  The bee drinks your health in the purest of dew ;

The lark has been waiting to sing you a song,
Which he practised in Cloudland on purpose for you!

"Come, come! you are either too bashful or lazy!
Lady Spring made this season an early entrée;
And she wonder'd what could have become of her Daisy;
We'll call you coquettish, if still you delay!"

Then a still, small voice, in the heart of the flower,
It was Instinct, whisper'd her, "Do not go!
You had better be quiet, and wait your hour;
It isn't too late even yet for snow!"

But the little field-blossom was foolish and vain,
And she said to herself, "What a belle I shall be!"
So she sprang to the light, as she broke from her chain,
And gayly she cried, "I am free! I am free!"

A shy little thing is the Daisy, you know;
And she was half frighten'd to death, when she found

Not a blossom had even *begun* to blow!
  How she wish'd herself back again under the ground!

The tear in her timid and sorrowful eye
  Might well put the zephyr and beam to the blush;
But the saucy light laugh'd, and said, "Pray don't cry!"
  And the gay zephyr sang to her, "Hush, sweet, hush!"

They kiss'd her and petted her fondly at first;
  But a storm arose, and the false light fled;
And the zephyr changed into angry breeze,
  That scolded her till she was almost dead!

The gem on her bosom was stain'd and dark,
  The snow of her robe had lost its light,
And tears of sorrow had dimm'd the spark
  Of beauty and youth, that made her bright!

And so she lay with her fair head low,
  And mournfully sigh'd in her dying hour,
"Ah! had I courageously answer'd 'no!'
  I had now been safe in my native bower!"

THE LIFE-VOYAGE.

A BALLAD.

Once in the olden time there dwelt,
  Beside the sounding sea,
A little maid—her garb was coarse,
  Her spirit pure and free.

Her parents were an humble twain,
  And poor as poor could be;
Yet gayly sang the guileless child,
  Beside the sounding sea.

The hut was bare, and scant the fare,
  And hard her little bed;
But she was rich! A single gem
  Its beauty round her shed.

She walk'd in light!—'twas all her wealth—
  That pearl, whose lustrous glow
Made her white forehead dazzling fair,
  And pure as sunlit snow.

Her parents died! With tears she cried,
  "God will my father be!"
Then launch'd alone her shallop light,
  And bravely put to sea.

The sail she set was virgin-white,
  As inmost lily leaf,
And angels whisper'd her from Heaven,
  To loose it or to reef.

And ever on the dancing prow
  One glorious brilliant burn'd,
By whose clear ray she read her way,
  And every danger learn'd:

For she had hung her treasure there,
  Her heaven-illumined pearl!
And so she steer'd her lonely bark,
  That fair and guileless girl!

The wind was fresh, the sails were free,
High dash'd the diamond spray,
And merrily leaping o'er the sea,
The light skiff left the bay!

But soon false, evil spirits came,
And strove, with costly lure,
To bribe her maiden heart to shame,
And win her jewel pure.

They swarm'd around the fragile boat,
They brought her diamonds rare,
To glisten on her graceful throat,
And bind her flowing hair!

They brought her gold from Afric-land,
And from the sea-king's throne
They pilfer'd gems, to grace her hand
And clasp her virgin zone.

But still she shook the silken curl
Back from her beaming eyes,
And cried—" I bear my spotless pearl
Home, home to yonder skies!

"Now shame ye not your ocean gems
  And Eastern gold to show?
Behold! how mine outburns them all!
  God's smile is in its glow!"

Fair blows the wind, the sail swells free,
  High shoots the diamond spray,
And merrily o'er the murmuring sea
  The light boat leaps away!

They swarm'd around the fragile bark,
  They strove with costlier lure
To bribe her maiden heart to shame,
  And win her jewel pure.

"We bring thee rank—we bring thee power—
  We bring thee pleasures free—
No empress, in her silk-hung bower,
  May queen her realm like thee!

"Now yield us up the one white pearl!
  'Tis but a star, whose ray
Will fail thee, rash, devoted girl,
  When tempests cloud thy way."

But still she smiled a loftier smile,
  And raised her frank, bright eyes,
And cried—" I bear my vestal star
  Home, home to yonder skies!"

The wind is fresh—the sail swells free—
  High shoots the diamond spray!
And merrily o'er the moaning sea
  The light boat leaps away!

Suddenly, stillness broods around,
  A stillness as of death,
Above, below—no motion, sound!
  Hardly a struggling breath!

Then wild and fierce the tempest came,
  The dark wind-demons clash'd
Their weapons swift—the air was flame!
  The waves in madness dash'd!

They swarm'd around the tossing boat—
  " Wilt yield thy jewel *now?*
Look! look! already drench'd in spray,
  It trembles at the prow.

"Be *ours* the gem! and safely launch'd
  Upon a summer sea,
Where never cloud may frown in heaven,
  Thy pinnace light shall be!"

But still she smiled a fearless smile,
  And raised her trusting eyes,
And cried—"I bear my talisman
  Home, home to yonder skies!"

And safe through all that blinding storm
  The true bark floated on,
And soft its pearl-illumined prow
  Through all the tumult shone!

An angel, guided through the clouds
  By that most precious light,
Flew down the fairy helm to take,
  And steer the boat aright.

Then died the storm upon the sea!
  High dash'd the diamond spray,
And merrily leaping light and free,
  The shallop sail'd away.

And meekly, when at eve her bark
  Its destined port had found,
She moor'd it by the mellow spark
  Her jewel shed around!

Wouldst know the name the maiden wore?
  'Twas Innocence—like thine!
Wouldst know the pearl she nobly bore?
  'Twas Truth—a gem divine!

Thou hast the jewel—keep it bright,
  Undimm'd by mortal fear,
And bathe each stain upon its light
  With Grief's repentant tear!

Still shrink from falsehood's fairest guise,
  By flattery unbeguiled!
Still let thy heart speak from thine eyes,
  My pure and simple child!

THE CHILD AND ITS ANGEL-PLAYMATE.

"My child! thou droopest like a flower
That trembles 'neath the summer shower,
And day by day, and hour by hour,
  More faint thy meek replying
To tender questionings of mine;
A dreamy sorrow, half divine,
Fills those dark eyes, that strangely shine;
  My child, my child! thou'rt dying!"

"Sweet mother—no: but by my side,
Where'er I go," the child replied,
"Through all this glorious summer-tide,
  Is one you cannot see—
A little child with sunny wings,
And eyes like Heaven;—of holy things,
With earnest voice, it talks and sings—
  And softly plays with me!

"'Let us go home!' it warbles low;
And when I say—'I dare not so!
My home is here,' it whispers—'No!
  Fair child! thy home is mine!'
And then, of some far lovelier land
It fondly tells, where many a band
Of blissful children, hand in hand,
  With sportive fondness twine.

"It says they know not how to sigh,
For nothing there can droop and die;
But bloom immortal glads the eye,
  And music wondrous sweet
Doth ebb and flow, without alloy,
From lyres of light, while Love and Joy
Time to the tune, their blest employ,
  With weariless wingéd feet!

"A purer prayer it teaches me
Than that I idly learn'd of thee;
It softens all my thoughtless glee,
  It makes me true and kind.
My angel-playmate! most I fear,
'Twill wave its wings and leave me here!
'Thou'lt miss me in that holier sphere!
  Oh! leave me not behind!'

"It says *this* is not life, but death,
A daily waste of mortal breath,
And still its sweet voice summoneth
  Me to that other land;
But even while it whispers so,
The flowers around more brightly glow,
And yet—and yet, I pine to go,
  And join that joyous band!

"My mother! I'll come often back;
I'll not forget the homeward track,
But oft when Pain and Sorrow rack
  Thy frame, I'll hover o'er thee;
I'll sing thee every soothing lay
I learn in heaven;—I'll lead the way
For thee to God;—my wings shall play
  In dreams of light before thee!

"Oh! mother! even now I hear
Melodious murmurs in my ear;
The child—the angel-child is near!
  I see its light wings glow!
I see its pure and pleading smile!
It moves beside me all the while,
Its eyes my yearning soul beguile,
  Sweet mother! let me go!

"Hark to their plaintive spirit-strain!
'Let us go home!' again—again
It rises soft—that sad refrain!
My playmate! stay for me!
It clasps my hand! It warbles low—
'Let us go home!' I go—I go!
My pinions play—with heavenly glow—
My mother—I am free!"

The fair child lay upon her breast,
As if in its accustom'd rest,
A slumbering dove within its nest.
But well the mother knew
That never more that pure blue eye
To hers would speak the soul's reply;
"She is not *dead*—she could not *die!*
My child in heaven! adieu!"

A SONG.

Yes! "lower to the level"
  Of those who laud thee now!
Go! join the joyous revel,
  And pledge the heartless vow!
Go! dim the soul-born beauty
  That lights that lofty brow!
Fill, fill the bowl! let burning wine
Drown, in thy soul, Love's dream divine!

Yet when the laugh is lightest,
  When wildest goes the jest,
When gleams the goblet brightest,
  And proudest heaves thy breast,
And thou art madly pledging
  Each gay and jovial guest,—
A ghost shall glide amid the flowers—
The shade of Love's departed hours!

And thou shalt shrink in sadness
From all the splendor there,
And curse the revel's gladness,
And hate the banquet's glare,
And pine, 'mid Passion's madness,
For true Love's purer air,
And feel thou'dst give their wildest glee
For one unsullied sigh from me!

Yet deem not this my prayer, love,
Ah! no! if I could keep
Thy alter'd heart from care, love,
And charm its griefs to sleep,
Mine only should despair, love,
I—I alone would weep!
I—I alone would mourn the flowers
That fade in Love's deserted bowers!

A MOTHER'S PRAYER IN ILLNESS.

YES! take them first, my Father! Let my doves
Fold their white wings in Heaven, safe on thy breast,
Ere I am call'd away! I dare not leave
Their young hearts here, their innocent, thoughtless
hearts!
Ah! how the shadowy train of future ills
Comes sweeping down life's vista as I gaze!
My May! my careless, ardent-temper'd May!
My frank and frolic child! in whose blue eyes
Wild joy and passionate wo alternate rise;
Whose cheek, the morning in her soul illumes;
Whose little, loving heart, a word, a glance,
Can sway to grief or glee; who leaves her play,
And puts up her sweet mouth and dimpled arms,
Each moment for a kiss, and softly asks,
With her clear, flute-like voice, "Do you love me?"
Ah! let me stay! ah! let me still be by,

To answer her and meet her warm caress!
For I away, how oft in this rough world,
That earnest question will be ask'd in vain!
How oft that eager, passionate, petted heart,
Will shrink abash'd and chill'd, to learn at length
The hateful, withering lesson of distrust!
Ah! let her nestle still upon this breast,
In which each shade, that dims her darling face,
Is felt and answer'd, as the lake reflects
The clouds that cross yon smiling heaven! and thou—
My modest Ellen! tender, thoughtful, true;
Thy soul attuned to all sweet harmonies;
My pure, proud, noble Ellen! with thy gifts
Of genius, grace, and loveliness, half hidden
'Neath the soft veil of innate modesty,
How will the world's wild discord reach thy heart
To startle and appal! thy generous scorn
Of all things base and mean—thy quick, keen taste,
Dainty and delicate—thy instinctive fear
Of those unworthy of a soul so pure,
Thy rare, unchildlike dignity of mien,
All—they will all bring pain to thee, my child!
And oh! if even their grace and goodness meet
Cold looks and careless greetings, how will all
The latent *evil* yet undisciplined

In their young, timid souls, forgiveness find ?
Forgiveness, and forbearance, and soft chidings,
Which I—their mother—learn'd of Love to give!
Ah! let me stay!—albeit my heart is weary,
Weary and worn, tired of its own sad beat,
That finds no echo in this busy world
Which cannot pause to answer—tired alike
Of joy and sorrow—of the day and night!
Ah! take them first, my Father! and then me;
And for their sakes—for their sweet sakes, my
Father!
Let me find rest beside them, at thy feet!

TO ——.

Let your summer friends go by
With the summer weather!
Hearts there are that will not fly,
Tho' the storm should gather.

Summer love to fortune clings,
 From the *wreck* it saileth,
Like the bee, that spreads its wings
 When the honey faileth.

Rich the soil where weeds appear ;—
 Let their false bloom perish !
Flowers there are, more rare and dear,
 That you still may cherish.

Flowers of feeling, pure and warm,
 Hearts that cannot wither,
These for thee shall bide the storm,
 As the sunny weather.

THE TRIUMPH OF THE SPIRITUAL OVER THE SENSUAL.

AN ALLEGORY.

NEAR a being on the verge of manhood,
  In a waking vision, I behold
Two fair figures,—one is lowly kneeling,
  At his feet, with loosen'd locks of gold,
Down her white, half-veilèd bosom, stealing,
  O'er her warm cheek, in soft tresses, roll'd,
Link'd with many a burning gem, revealing
  Radiant colors through each silken fold.

One soft, dimpled hand uplifts a chalice,
  Richly chased, and starr'd with rubies rare,
While the other points towards a palace,
  Rising like a dream upon the air!

Wild blue eyes, where passion blends with malice,
Red, ripe lips,—Temptation triumphs there!
Or if thence the tried heart proudly rallies,
In her *form*, voluptuously fair,
Grace, so tenderly alluring, dallies,
With her captive, that he loves the snare.
Loose her gorgeous robe, her feet are bare!—
Thus the charmer sings, with wooing air,—

Taste the goblet! beauteous mortal!
Quickly taste, and fly with me!
Yonder gleams the golden portal
Of a mansion made for thee.
There will Pleasure's downy pillow
Woo thee to luxurious rest;
There will Trouble's stormy billow
Never fret thy charmèd breast!
Beauty there shall bless the hours,
Flitting by on balmy wing;
Joy shall bind thy brow with flowers;
Hope of new delights shall sing.
Drain the goblet! beauteous mortal!
Quickly drain! and fly with me!
Yonder gleams the radiant portal
Of the mansion wrought for thee!

From his trance of rapture, wildly waking,
Lo! the lost, infatuated boy,
Flush'd with hope, the fatal chalice taking,
Bends to quaff,—his ruin, in his joy!
Hark! those tones, melodiously breaking
O'er his soul, the sinful spell destroy!

Turning now, he sees a veilèd vision,
That has stood beside him all the while;
Beauty dawning, with a light elysian,
Through the snowy gauze, as morning's smile
Glows and glistens 'neath her wreathèd mist,
All the lovelier for that shade, I wist.

Veil'd from head to foot,—her fair arms folding
With a sweet composure on her breast,
And a cross of pearl, serenely holding
In her hand, with tender reverence press'd:

One soft-gleaming star, amid the braiding
Of her raven hair, her brow illumes;
Beautiful, exceedingly, the shading
Of the rose, that on her pure cheek blooms!

Like the music-fall of water playing,
Freshly in the burning summer-tide,

With delicious melody, allaying
All his feverish ecstasy and pride—

Thrilling, low, unutterably sweet,
Came her pure, soft tones, with angel pleading,
While his heart to each clear cadence beat,
Quick, in glad reply, all else unheeding.

Boy, refrain! the poison, breathing
From the goblet, clouds thy soul!
Lo! the golden serpent, wreathing
Round the brim with glittering roll,
Emblem of the death within,
Know'st thou not it tempts to sin?

Boy, beware! *I* may not offer
Joy unearn'd by toil of thine;
Wealth, with lock'd and laden coffer,
Luxury's pillow are not mine.
But if thou, with trust confiding,
High and fervent walk with me,
Holiest comfort—peace abiding,
Thine thro' trials dark, shall be!
Like the mystic steps in air,
That th' Egyptian pupil trod,

Fast as one wish fades, a higher
  Shall but lead thee nearer God!

Boy, be mine! beneath our feet
  Desert wastes shall bloom with flowers,
Sorrow's self shall seem most sweet,
  While Hope's rainbow lights her showers.

Troops of angels, only known
  By their choral music-tide,
(Ebb and flow) with softest tone,
  Shall beside thee viewless glide!

Every warbler of the wild-wood
  On its voice shall waft thy soul,
Back thro' all the dreams of childhood,
  To the Heaven-home whence it stole.

From each blossom Spring shall bring thee
  Some sweet lesson thou'lt command,
Even the winding shell shall sing thee
  Echoes from the spirit-land!

Glory waits thee, glad immortal!
  Take thy cross and go with me!

Stars shall light the viewless portal
Of the mansion made for thee!

Softly, with that last word, died away
Voice and vision, from my dreaming sense;
But the youth rose, ere she closed the lay,
And with eyes illumed by thought intense,
Placed his hand in hers, that she should lead him thence.

PURITY'S PEARL;

OR, THE HISTORY OF A TEAR.

A MAIDEN, one summer's day, over Life's sea,
In a pleasure-boat swiftly sailing,
Gazed back on the bowers of her childhood free,
That were dim in the distance failing.
She had clasp'd her zone with a brilliant stone,
In tint like the plume of a Lory,
Through its heart the blush of the dawn had shone,
And left it in all its glory.

"False, false the talisman!" cries the girl,
  "From my bosom the gem I sever!
Oh! give me back purity's snow-white pearl,
  And away with Love's Ruby for ever!"
A tear, as she spoke, dimm'd her eye's blue fire,
  And fell in the foaming water,
And hark! at the moment, an angel-lyre
  Sounds the name of earth's sorrowing daughter:—
'Tis the spirit of mercy floats from Heaven,
  Like light thro' the waves descending,
And the penitent feels her fault forgiven,
  While smiles with her tears are blending.
And long ere that frail bark reach'd the shore,
  Fair Mercy, her pledge redeeming,
Stole up thro' the moonlit sea once more,
  With a pearl in her soft hand beaming.
"I bring thee back Purity's gem of Snow!
  'Tis thy tear of remorse and devotion,
Transform'd to a pearl, in the wondrous flow
  Of Time's mysterious ocean."
And the maiden has bound her zone again,
  With the treasure she prized so truly,
And safe is her bark on the fathomless main,
  For her talisman keeps it holy!

TO ——.

You are not what you used to be,
  When we were merry girls;
Your hair,—that floated then so free,
  In wild aerial curls,

Or drooping, from your forehead meek,
  In beautiful repose,—
Lay light and soft upon your cheek—
  A shadow on the rose!—

Is parted, with Madonna grace,
  Above a sadden'd brow,
And shades a calm and thoughtful face,
  That wears no rose-bloom now!

You are not what you used to be;
  Your girlhood's lightsome mood,
Your springing step and tone of glee,
  Are soften'd and subdued.

You are not what you used to be ;
  But oh ! how much more worth,
Than that light thing of frolic free,
  The wildest girl on earth !

Forever—as the joyous play
  Of bloom and light has faded,
And tint by tint, and ray by ray,
  By care has been o'ershaded,—

You have been gathering holier wealth
  Within—a store of-treasures !
Flowers, fairer than the Rose of Health,
  And rays, more rich than Pleasure's !

And while the worthless splendor stole,
  Unheeded, from those eyes,
A lamp was lighted in your soul—
  A star that never dies !

You are not what you used to be ;
  But you are less of earth,
And richer, in your want of glee,
  Than others, in their mirth !

LINES FROM A SCHOOL-GIRL TO A NEW FRIEND.

Will you let me love you, Fanny?
  There are very few
In my soul's still temple cherish'd—
  May it cherish you?
Many make a fleeting visit,
  Wearying ere long—
Far too wild and dreamy is it,
  For the worldly throng.

But if you will come and rest
  In its dim recesses,
It will give its stranger-guest
  Welcome and caresses.
Gentle is the group you'll meet;
  Pray do not refuse them;
They will always love you, sweet;
  Let me introduce them!

You will see their faces only—
   Angels are drawn so ;
And the heart makes angels ever
   Of its friends, you know.
One with eyes like starlit clouds,
   Beautiful as truth,
In whose face her rich soul smiles
   With undying youth.

Then with brown and braided hair,
   Head of classic grace,
Brow serene, and tranquil eyes,
   Comes a seraph face.
You can see that she has sorrow'd,
   From the world apart :
Pure and lovely as her forehead,
   So the maiden's heart.

Next with glance upraised, inspired,
   Music in her eyes,
Soft in grief—in passion fired—
   See Julie arise !
On her cheek unearthly bloom ;
   Round her brow so fair,

Glossy as a raven's plume,
  Sweeps her wealth of hair.

Next appears my pride and idol,
  One, within whose soul
Love and Truth have met in bridal,
  Free from earth's control.
Guileless, trusting as a child,
  Playful, dauntless, daring,
Full of romance, high and wild,
  Ne'er in wo despairing !

Far apart from all and hidden—
  Frowning on them too,
There is one, who came unbidden,
  That is—you know who !
Now you'll let me love you, Fanny !
  Since you see how few
In my heart's far depths are treasured,
  Let it treasure you !

HEAVEN IS OVER ALL.

In weary paths, my precious boy,
  Your faltering feet must fall;
But bear in mind, where'er you go,
  That Heaven is over all!

You're tripping thro' a garden now,
  Where childhood loves to play,
And kind hands pull the flowers for you,
  And throw the thorns away;

And softly falls the tender light—
  The breeze—'tis joy to breathe it!
And if, perchance, a shower descends,
  New blossoms wake beneath it;

But by and by you'll leave your bower,
  And "go your ways" alone,
With but a chance companion, love,
  Across your pathway thrown;

And sometimes in the desert bare,
  Grief's bitter tears must fall;
But bear in mind, my boy, e'en there,
  That Heaven is over all!

And sometimes over flinty rocks
  Your tender feet must stray;
And sometimes in a tangled wood
  You'll almost lose your way;

And oft you'll sigh for Childhood's home,
  When gloomy scenes appal,—
Oh! bear in mind, where'er you roam,
  That Heaven is over all!

Be sure a sunbeam, thro' that wood,
  Will light you on your way;
Be sure, within that solitude,
  Some living fount will play.

And tho' the flinty rock should fret
  Full long your weary feet,
There's moss upon its bosom yet,
  Will make a pillow sweet:

And now and then a balmy air
  Will float with soft perfume,
And lovely blossoms, here and there,
  Will bless you with their bloom:

But if the clouds should hide the sky,
  And blinding rain should fall,
Remember, God is always nigh,
  And Heaven is over all!

Now—now, while yet in Childhood's bower,
  With that wild way in view,
Oh! *put your little hand in His*,
  And He will lead you through!

For if, with pure and patient heart,
  With firm resolve and high,
You tread the path appointed, love,
  And pass Temptation by,

A fairer home than Childhood's home,
  A fonder love than ours,
Await you at your journey's end,
  In Heaven's own balmy bowers.

Where'er you go—in weal or wo,
 Whatever fate befall,
In sunny glade, in forest shade,
 A *Heaven is over all!*

THE MORNING WALK, OR THE STOLEN BLUSH.

A LOVER'S LAY.

NEVER tell me that cheek is not painted, false maid!
 'Tis a fib, tho' your pretty lip pouts while I say it;
And if the cheat were not already betray'd,
 Those exquisite blushes themselves would betray it.

But listen! this morning you rose ere the dawn,
 To keep an appointment perhaps—with Apollo?
And finding a fairy foot-print on the lawn,
 Which I could not mistake, I determined to fol-
  low.

To the hill-side I track'd it, and tripping above me,
Her sun-ringlets flying and jewell'd with dew,
A maiden I saw!—now the truth, if you love me—
But why should I question—I'm sure it was you!

And you cannot deny you were met in ascending,—
I meanwhile pursuing my truant by stealth,—
By a blooming young seraph, who turn'd, and attending
Your steps, said her name was "the Spirit of Health."

Meantime, thro' the mist of transparent vermilion
That suddenly flooded the brow of the hill,
All fretted with gold, rose Aurora's pavilion,
Illumining meadow, and mountain, and rill.

And Health, floating up through the luminous air,
Dipp'd her fingers of snow in those clouds glowing bright;
Then turn'd and dash'd down, o'er her votary fair,
A handful of rose-beams that bathed her in light.

Even yet they're at play here and there in your form,
Thro' your fingers they steal to the white taper tips,

Now rush to that cheek its soft dimples to warm,
  Now deepen the crimson that lives in your lips.

Will you tell me again, with that scorn-lighted eye,
  That you do not use paint—while such tinting is
        there ?
While the glow still affirms what the glance would
        deny ?
  No ! in future disclaim the sweet theft if you dare !

THE HALF-BLOWN ROSE.

SUGGESTED BY A PORTRAIT.

'Tis just the flower she ought to wear,—
  The simple flower the painter chose ;
And are they not a charming pair—
  The modest girl—the half-blown rose ?

The glowing bud has stolen up
  With tender smile and blushing grace,
And o'er its mossy clasping cup
  In bashful pride reveals its face.

The maiden too, with timid feet,
  Has sprung from childhood's verdant bower,
And lightly left its limit sweet,
  For woman's lot of shine and shower.

See ! from its veil of silken hair,
  That bathes her cheek in clusters bright,
Her sweet face, like a blossom fair,
  Reveals its wealth of bloom and light.

How softly blends with childhood's smile
  That maiden-mien of pure repose !
Oh ! seems she not herself the while—
  A breathing flower—a half-blown rose ?

THE HOUR BEFORE THE DUEL.

Too late—too late—ye steal before me,
  Fond thoughts of home, of love and joy!
The wings of fate close darkening o'er me—
  Oh God! my wife! my boy!

My own sweet wife! I see thy face—
  Thy pure, young face upraised to mine,
Thy glossy ringlets' waving grace,
  Thy blush, thy smile divine!

Thy pleading eyes, that droop'd like flowers
  Beneath a cloud, when I was cold—
Oh! to win back the wasted hours,
  My brief life's lavish'd gold!

My child! my heart's own hope and pride,
  My dark-eyed, blooming, glorious boy!
Thou comest—Heaven! in mercy hide
  That gaze of thoughtless joy!

Yes, Honor! 'gainst thine idle name,
A bubble that a breath may break,
To 'scape the knave's or fool's false blame,
THEIR happiness I stake.

I yield to thee my hope, my love,
HER life that yet in joy has smiled,
My peace on earth—my bliss above—
Oh God! my wife and child!

I'll dream no more! I'll nerve my soul—
Hurrah! the wild—the magic wine!
Fill up—fill high—the glorious bowl!
Drown care in draughts divine!

The past—the future! hence, away!
Fears, dreams, and doubts—my spirit's strife—
I dare not think, or feel, or pray—
Oh God! my boy—my wife!

SHE SAYS SHE LOVES ME DEARLY.

A SONG.

SHE says her heart is in her kiss—
  She says she loves me dearly;
Why meet I not her tenderness
  As fondly, as sincerely?

Ah! *once* I trusted all I met,
  With warm and artless truth;
And once my words were from my soul,
  But that was in my youth.

And trust betray'd, and vows forgot,
  And wrong return'd for kindness,
Have chill'd my heart, and changed my lot,
  And cured my blissful blindness.

No longer tender, guileless, meek,
  Confiding as the dove,
Too oft I think before I speak,
  And *doubt* before I love!

THE HERO'S GRAVE.

A GROUP of boys in playful strife—
  A soldier old and faded,—
The fresh and glowing morn of life,—
  The eve serenely shaded.—

"Ah! play not there, my children!
  I pray you play not there!"
He spoke with tears,—that weary one,—
  The man with silver hair.

"And why?" the thoughtless children said,—
  "The grass is fresher here,

We love upon the mound to tread,
  And what have we to fear?"

" Nay, come away!" he raised his voice,
  Wild flash'd his faded eyes,
" Ye sport upon a hallow'd grave,
  For there *a hero lies!*"

THE END.

www.ingramcontent.com/pod-product-compliance
Lightning Source LLC
LaVergne TN
LVHW010254110826
845151LV00004B/1471

* 9 7 8 1 4 2 5 5 2 1 9 4 3 *